WALKING
IN THE FATHER'S RICHES

THE PROSPERITY OF SONSHIP

FRED & SHERRY WHITE

Find this book online for free on many open source book platforms. Why? Because we want everyone to read it.

Find it online in every ebook format for digital readers at www.bookshooter.com--where the independent author can finally go digital!

This book was created via a partnership with www.TheEmpowermentHouse.com--a coaching service for the author who wants to be profitably independent.

Published by Fountain Gate Publishers
Athens, GA USA
www.FountainGatePublishers.com

Cover Design: Kyle Steed

Printed in the Unites States of America

ISBN: 978-0-615-34349-5
Library of Congress Number: 2009944050

Dedicated to Our Parents

We embrace family as one of the most important things in a person's life. Through the ministry, we have observed the importance of family. The impact of loving parents is beyond measure. Praying mothers pull children out of the fires of hell. Fathers set direction in the lives of their children. I have observed that over 90 percent of wealthy people were positively influenced by their fathers. Less than 30 percent of the people in jails and prisons were positively influenced by their fathers. Less than 10 percent of the homeless people living on the streets knew their fathers.

Sherry's parents, J.L .and Jean Stevens, have been a blessing to our family. JL gave Sherry the ability to overcome and the courage to face any situation in life. Jean gave Sherry love and a strong will that helps fortify and propel her to reach her goals.

My parents, F.W. and Ola White, provided the finances and other support for Sherry and me to pursue higher education. We are especially thankful for their love and help. My dad inspired the drive and determination in me, while my mother gave me refinement and sensitivity. After my mother's death, my dad married Louise, who I love as a mother. She showed God's love to me and my family.

Our spiritual father, Brother Bob Terrell, brought us into spiritual family and released us into the work of God. He imparted to us a revelation of the body of Christ and the understanding that we stand on foundation and move forward in revelation.

Fred and Sherry White

TABLE OF CONTENTS

FORWARD

Sherry and I (Fred) are high school sweethearts who have enjoyed over 45 years of marriage together. We plan to be together forever and a day! Our ministry together so far has had several different expressions. We taught children, youth and adults in different local congregations until we met our spiritual father, Bob Terrell. Brother Bob birthed destiny in us and separated us for the work of God for which we were called. Then the Lord began to open up doors to us to bring the ministry gift to the people.

Jesus spoke to me in 1982 saying, "I will make you rich, and I want you to teach My people how to be rich." My response to the call of Jesus was that I did not want to proclaim the same message of prosperity that others used to exploit God's people. Their message implied that only the rich could purchase prosperity. Jesus responded to me, "Have you never read how I prospered Joseph in prison?" Joseph prospered because the Lord was with him (Genesis 39:2). The Holy Spirit began to reveal the truth to me that Jesus Christ prospers people, regardless of their circumstances. He will prosper those in jails, prisons and in the direst of situations.

At the age of nine, Sherry was called by Jesus to go into all the world and preach the gospel to every creature. Later, Jesus spoke to Sherry saying, "I call you Israel for you have power with Me." Along with authority and power comes responsibility to be an example and an ambassador for Christ. God's power heals, delivers and sets people free. Since the time the Lord spoke to Sherry, she has been going from city to city and village to village preaching, teaching, and healing. The Lord spoke to her on a plane going to Texas and told her to watch her words carefully because they had creative power.

So, in the 1980s we both had a call of God on our lives. To prepare, we submitted to the Lord's authority, studied the word of God and received from anointed ministers. In the 1990s we had a revelation. We taught the revelation of Jesus Christ in many different venues in this country and elsewhere. We started teaching children in low income areas. Then we had a mission for homeless people, prostitutes and addicts in our city for eight years. We financed the mission and other ministry activities until others came alongside us to help. We ministered in different congregations, homes, jails and prisons. We saw Jesus heal, deliver and set the people free. He prospered the people in all areas of life. Now we have a story. Our story tells how Jesus has changed the lives of people. This book explains the revelation that the Holy Spirit has given us and it tells our story.

We began writing together professionally in the 1970s. We were prompted by the Holy Spirit to write this book together when we saw how Jesus used our ministry to change the lives of people who had been in poverty and bondage. The message is for anyone who needs insight and help in their walk with the Father and in receiving His riches. Though I will write this book in my own voice, I will include many of Sherry's prophetic words, insights and suggestions.

I would like to shed some preliminary light on the purposes of this book. God's children have been deceived and exploited in the area of finances. They have fallen for many false doctrines in the area of prosperity. They looked for the spectacular and missed the supernatural. They built religious institutions rather than godly relationships. They substituted formulas for a relationship with the Lord. They followed steps that led nowhere, and prospered themselves but not God. They focused on current circumstances and forfeited their influence over the future. They desired the crumbs when they could be feasting at the banqueting table. This book exposes these deceptions and many others that have been used to rob God's children. Even in their lack, they have known that God has abundance for them. They have just not been able to tap into His abundance. They have lacked knowledge concerning the operation of God's abundance. There is a generation coming forth that will not be deceived or manipulated. Instead, they will be armed with the truth that will set them free. This book uncovers the deceptions and shows how to prosper in God's economy.

The new season is the Age of Revelation. The Holy Spirit is revealing Jesus and the Lord's will to navigate through perilous times. Trust in the Lord and be led by His Spirit in everything for the things that worked in the past will not work in this season. Do not let your trust be in this world's economy, because the Lord shows mercy to those who trust Him. Even when the world's economy is turned upside down, believers who trust in the Lord and are led by the Spirit will prosper.

This book is intended for those people who are hungry for the truth about God's economy and finances. It is not intended for those people who are set in their ways and satisfied with traditions of men and the current situation. They will easily dismiss what the Holy Spirit is saying to the Church. The purpose of the book is to help you prosper in your spirit, soul, body and finances. If you read the book with an open heart, the Holy Spirit will shine light on misconceptions in your life that will set you free. Furthermore, He will encourage you to make any changes needed in your life so that you can walk in abundance in every area of your life.

As to the organization of this book, it is comprised of three sections: foundation, godly living and touching the eternal. First, the foundation section digs up the roots of financial problems and lays a sure foundation. The first chapter identifies the roots of persistent poverty and debt and provides solutions. These roots have to be dealt with before the foundation can be laid and financial freedom can be achieved. Chapter 2 shows how the old mindset will not work in the new season. It lays the foundation of love and of faith that is based on the word of God and a Spirit-led life. Chapter 3 shows the importance of a strong personal relationship with the Heavenly Father.

Second, the godly living section examines an overcoming lifestyle. Chapter 4 introduces the kingdom spirit, which places priority on loving King Jesus and caring for His people. Chapter 5 shows how believers can fashion their future by giving the best off the top. Chapter 6 examines the characteristics and actions of good stewards.

Third, the section on touching the eternal shows how heaven responds to a Spirit-led believer operating in love and faith. Operating in the supernatural arena is what God wants for His people. Chapter 7 examines how the Lord moves through His economy to affect lives on the earth. Chapter 8 shows how to receive and impart eternal legacies. Chapter 9 culminates the book by calling for intimate fellowship with the Lord Jesus Christ.

Chapter 1

FINANCIAL FREEDOM FOR THE FAMILY

In the world's system, all debt can be separated into two broad categories. The first type of debt can be placed in the "ability-to-pay" category, meaning that debt is owed by people with the ability to pay it. People with the ability to pay may borrow strategically to buy such things as a house or an automobile. They may borrow to invest in real estate or education. There would generally be no real problems associated with this category of debt, because the people have the ability to repay the debt.

The second type of debt can be placed in the "inability-to-pay" category. In such cases, people who are unable to pay may feel under pressure to borrow in times of emergencies such as sickness or unemployment. Some may borrow in one time period thinking that they will be able to repay later as their situation improves. When circumstances do not improve as planned, these people may be unable to pay the debt that has already been incurred. Unwanted debt may also arise from the attacks of your enemies–the devil, the world or the flesh. Clearly, this second category of debt is unwanted and burdensome and has significant problems associated with it. Despite the natural approaches of dealing with this type of debt, like budgeting and planning for repayment, it is beyond the ability of the debtors to pay.

Since natural approaches to this problematic type of debt do not work and will never work, this chapter turns to biblical approaches to solve it. While many people successfully handle debt for which they have an ability to pay, only God specializes in eliminating debt for people who are unable to pay. God sent His Son to redeem us from a debt that we could not pay. On several occasions, Jesus taught about borrowers who were unable to pay their debts: "A moneylender had two debtors: one owed five hundred denarii, and the other fifty. When they were unable to repay, he graciously forgave them both" (Luke 7:41-42a).

Even though they were unable to pay, their debts were eliminated. These scriptures offer hope for those with debt that they cannot pay. This chapter will address only the "inability-to-pay" category of debt, and so any further reference to debt implicitly refers to that category. The objective of the chapter is to help achieve financial freedom for those people who do not have the ability to pay off their debt.

The inheritance that I received when my dad passed away was a large debt. During my dad's lifetime, he was not able to pay off one particular debt. The creditor wanted to take everything that he owned in payment for that debt. His debt simply grew larger and larger every year. It was much more than my family could possibly pay. I called on the Lord, and He was merciful. My family was able to sell one property for a mere fraction of the debt and settle the entire account with the creditor. My family was able to keep other properties with a clear title. The favor of both the Heavenly Father and man was on my family.

While this debt reduction was a miracle from the Heavenly Father, it gave guidance to Sherry and me in another area of our lives that concerned debt. When we were a young married couple, we did not always tithe. Later, it concerned us that we had not paid what belonged to the Father. We asked the Father to reduce the debt that resulted from our unpaid tithes. He placed the same amount for debt reduction in both of our hearts. This was to be the amount of money that should be paid in order to clear these past debts. It was a much smaller amount than we owed. We were thankful for the mercy which the Father showed us in reducing the debt. We gladly paid the amount which He proposed, and our consciences were clear of this hindrance in our relationship with the Father. The Father wants all hindrances which limit your relationship with Him to be eliminated.

The devil can attack your finances in many different ways (1 Peter 5:8-9). Deception is one of his main tools against believers. First, the enemy wants you to think that you can solve your problems on your own, but Jesus said without Him you can do nothing (John 15:5). Second, the enemy wants you to think that your situation is hopeless, but Jesus said all things are possible to believers (Mark 9:23).

Furthermore, the enemy works in hidden ways, so the root or basic causes of the problems often are not readily apparent. The different root causes for persistent debt must be identified and dealt with in an appropriate manner in order to ensure financial freedom. In solving financial problems, a major deception comes from addressing only surface issues. Financial problems have not been solved effectively in the church world, because deceptive approaches have been used there, as well. Root causes of people's debt are often ignored so that ministers can focus on lucrative ways to raise finances. Many ministers on television programs tell people to plant a "seed" to eliminate their debt. However, no single solution works with every root. People who are living in sin with pride, prejudice, greed or unforgiveness cannot buy their way out of debt by simply planting a financial seed. They have to deal with the problem of sin. Using a simplistic, single approach such as planting a "seed" to deal with multiple root causes is bound to fail and subsequently injure many in the body of Christ. This simplistic approach is a way to raise money for ministers, but it does not help the vast majority of people. Heart issues must first be addressed. People are helped when root causes of debt are identified and destroyed.

Roots of Persistent Poverty and Debt

When a person sins his/her equity or ownership in the supernatural economy diminishes and debt increases. In the Lord's Prayer, Jesus taught that the concepts of sin and debt are closely related and can be interchanged: Luke's account of the Lord's Prayer includes the phrase "forgive us our sins" (Luke 11:4). The related phrase in Matthew's account is "forgive us our debts" (Matthew 6:12). Sin is a debt because it demands payment by way of punishment: "The wages of sin are death" (Romans 6:23). Sinners are sold into slavery under the control of sin (Romans 7:14). The word "iniquity," another word for sin, literally means no equity. A person with no equity or ownership has only liabilities or obligations to pay. Hence, committing inequities or sins causes a person to have debt in the spiritual realm.

Root causes of persistent poverty and debt are identified below. Some specific approaches to destroy these roots are briefly discussed.

Pride, Prejudice and Poverty Spirit

A biblical example of unwanted debt is the widow who needed to pay her late husband's debt (2 Kings 4:1-7). If she did not pay the debt, her sons would be forced into bondage by the creditor. This illustrates that families suffer the consequences of debt. As she sought help from the prophet Elisha, she revealed her attitude. She expected help from the Lord on the basis of the good deeds of her husband (his service to Elisha) and the fact that he reverenced the Lord (verse 1). Her statement reflected a religious attitude, wanting to exchange performance on earth for heaven's blessings. Both pride and prejudice were implied in her statement. She implied that she deserved help because her family was associated with the right group and did the right things. Since she had nothing of value except a little oil, she was under bondage to a poverty spirit, as well. She did not cry out for God's mercy, which is freely given. Instead she justified herself as she called for help.

Elisha spoke a prophetic word inspired by the Holy Spirit calling for her to act, which is called a prophetic call to action (verses 3-4). She had to borrow vessels from her neighbors, which would have been a humbling experience. Then she had to shut the door. Although we were not told why the door was to be shut, it appears that the door on ungodly attitudes was shut along with it. Then she was to pour the oil into the borrowed vessels. In obedience to the prophetic call to action, many vessels were borrowed and filled with oil. The supply of oil miraculously multiplied so that there was no lack. When all the vessels were filled, she sold the oil, paid the debt and used the rest to cover living expenses (verse 7). The widow could have ignored the prophet and died in her poverty. Instead, she obeyed the prophet and prospered: "Believe in the Lord your God and you shall be established; believe His prophets and you shall prosper" (2 Chronicles 20:20b NKJV). This story shows the impact of obeying a prophetic call to action. The door had to be shut to such things as pride, prejudice and a poverty spirit before prosperity could come to the widow and her family.

As we see in this story, one specific root of debt is pride. A person who is selfish and self-centered is proud. Such pride will lead to destruction (Proverbs 16:18). The Lord resists those who are proud (James 4:6). Pride causes people to think they have a better way of doing things than others. Therefore, they get frustrated when things are not done their way. People who stay depressed about the turmoil in their lives are self-centered and prideful. People who put themselves down may express false humility when they are really prideful.

In order to guard against pride, a person must humble himself/herself. Humility is not being weak or downcast, but it is casting all your cares on the Lord (1 Peter 5:6-7). Humility is an attitude about God rather than an attitude about yourself. Humility recognizes your dependence on God. It takes God's perspectives and adopts God's ways. You are not changed for the better by looking at you and your faults, even when you are trying to correct your faults. You are changed into the image of God's Son as you look into the face of Jesus.

Another specific root is prejudice. Prejudice involves thinking that other people are less than you. Making decisions about people based on such things as their appearance, speech, religion or economic status before knowing them is a sign of prejudice. Believers are not to judge others by forming their own opinions or their own perceptions (2 Corinthians 5:16). Prejudice is sin: "But if you show partiality, you are committing sin and are convicted by the law as transgressors" (James 2:9). Committing sin results in debt or obligations to pay through punishment (Romans 6:23). And Jesus paid the debt for sin by His death on the cross (Romans 8:2; Colossians 2:12-14).

Prejudice in the family of God is a direct result of immaturity. Paul addresses immaturity and prejudice in the first few chapters of 1 Corinthians. He described these Christians as carnal and babes in Christ (1 Corinthians 3:1). Envy, strife, divisions and factions were evident among them (1 Corinthians 3:3). These Christians divided themselves into factions on the basis of the leaders they believed and followed (1 Corinthians 1:12). Members of each faction thought their leader, and hence their group, was better than the others, which is a form of prejudice. This form of prejudice has been rampant in the body of Christ during the past season. The devil uses prejudice and division as devices to destroy believers. A house that is divided into factions cannot stand (Matthew 12:25; Luke 11:17). Immature people – those who hold prejudices – do not receive anything from the Holy Spirit (1 Corinthians 2:14). Failure to receive anything from the Holy Spirit results in poverty and often leads to persistent debt.

There is one family of God in heaven and earth (Romans 12:4-5; Ephesians 3:15). True leaders in the family of God do not divide the family into factions (1 Corinthians 3:4-6). When all members of the family are highly valued with none being considered unfavorably, the family is unified rather than divided. Real unity is based on love and preferring one another. When the family works together in unity to mature believers, it truly functions as God intended. As the family values and cares for all of its members, God blesses the family with increase. An increase from God will be manifested in every aspect of life, including finances.

Another specific root of debt we see in the story of the widow is the poverty spirit. A poverty spirit says "Get! Get! Get!" It is never satisfied. A poverty spirit is the absence of giving. It runs rampant through a family, stealing everything from it. Being under the control of a poverty spirit is like having holes in the money bags (Haggai 1:6). A poverty spirit can be present among any income group. It can even attach itself to rich people. Even people with millions of dollars can be driven by a poverty spirit to get more and hoard up. Jesus taught about a rich man who said, "I will tear down my barns and build larger ones, and there I will store all my grain and my goods' (Luke 12:18b). This attitude of hoarding is not being rich towards God (Luke 12:21).

A poverty spirit can affect every aspect of life. People in persistent poverty have low self esteem, thinking they are not worthy of more. They may be unable to keep decent jobs as a result. Families are poverty stricken when parents have no relationship with their children. Overcoming the poverty spirit is crucial to eliminating debt, and this unclean spirit is overcome with prayer and fasting (Matthew 17:21; Mark 9:29).

Greed

Greed is an excessive desire for money or power. Greed or the love of money is a root cause of many problems, including debt: "For the love of money is a root of all sorts of evil, and some by longing for it have wandered away from the faith and pierced themselves with many griefs" (1 Timothy 6:10).

The love of money and the things that money can buy cause people to stray from the faith and be troubled. Even people without money are subject to these problems if they love money. People who have money without loving it are not caught up in these problems. Jesus asked an important question of Peter that pertains to this subject and could be asked of all believers: "Do you love Jesus more than you love any of these things, including money and the things money can buy?" (John 21:15). Nothing should compare with your supreme love for Jesus.

The opposite of greed is generosity. Generosity gives, gives and gives! You can break off the root of greed by becoming generous in your giving: "Give and it will be given to you" (Luke 6:38a). Give your finances, time and effort as the Holy Spirit directs. If you love the Lord with all your heart and mind (Luke 10:27), your attitude towards finances will be to give generously. Generosity is the good that overcomes greed as a root of debt (Romans 12:21). As the root is destroyed, persistent debt withers.

Unforgiveness

If a person wrongs you, he/she may have to pay for the harm done. A driver who is responsible for a car accident could be obligated legally to pay for damages. However, many people harm others through their words and deeds without paying for the harm done. When you consider another person as being obligated to pay for his/her deeds against you, the perceived obligation becomes unforgiveness. As you release the obligation, it is forgiven.

The word of God teaches you to walk in the Spirit rather than in the natural realm. Harboring unforgiveness is natural, but forgiveness is an indication that you are walking in the Spirit. When you forgive the person who wrongs you, then you acknowledge that a wrong has been done and release your right to get even. Forgiveness is supernatural. By faith we forgive.

The love of God flowing through you counts no wrongs committed against you by any person (1 Corinthians 13:5). It does not take into account a wrong suffered. No matter what is done, love always forgives. "Be kind to one another, tender hearted, forgiving each other, just as God in Christ also has forgiven you" (Ephesians 4:32). Your motive to forgive everyone should be related to the forgiveness God showed by sacrificing His Son.

Jesus taught, "Forgive, and you will be forgiven" (Luke 6:37). No matter what you have done, God has forgiven you in Jesus Christ. He carried our guilt and our shame on the cross (Isaiah 53:4-5). Everything that was against us was nailed to the cross on which Jesus was crucified (Colossians 2:14). Even the records of our debts, trespasses and sins were completely eliminated. Unforgiveness binds you, but forgiveness frees you (Matthew 18:32-34).

As unforgiveness is dealt with one person at a time, forgiveness washes impurities away. Then your life is cleansed and prepared for the increase from heaven. As the flow from heaven increases in your life, persistent debt is eliminated.

Curse of Indebtedness

From a natural perspective, the genetic pool of your parents affects you. Also, the values, beliefs and actions of your parents and grandparents can influence you through the family environment in which you were raised. In particular, sin and evil in your family can adversely affect you. A root cause for persistent debt may be a generational curse resulting from the sins of parents and other ancestors (Exodus 20:4-5). Debt can arise from the curse of indebtedness (Deuteronomy 28:44-45). There is always a reason why people are cursed with indebtedness (Proverbs 26:2). Failure to obey the Lord is the general reason for being subject to a curse (Deuteronomy 28:15). The word of God shows that failure to forgive a brother (natural or spiritual) is a specific reason for the curse of indebtedness (Matthew 18:35).

If the curse of indebtedness gets a foothold in your family, it will stalk you, your children and their children after them. It has to be broken! Recognizing the curse is the first step in breaking it. The next step is to call it by name and destroy it with the blood of Jesus, the word of your testimony and laying down your life for Jesus (Revelation 12:11). As we read in Galatians 3:13a, "Christ redeemed us from the curse of the Law, having become a curse for us." With the curse destroyed, your family will be blessed above measure.

Walking in Financial Freedom

The previous section identified specific roots of persistent poverty and debt and provided guidance on dealing with these roots. This section examines general solutions to persistent poverty and debt and shows how to walk in financial freedom.

Jesus is the ultimate solution to the sin/debt problem. He shed His blood and died on the cross to pay the price for sin/debt (I Peter 1:18-19). When people make Jesus Christ their Lord and Savior and walk in the Spirit, they are freed from the law of sin and death: "Therefore there is now no condemnation for those who are in Christ Jesus. For the law of the Spirit of life in Christ Jesus has set you free from the law of sin and of death" (Romans 8:1-2). Jesus sets you free. Here are some ways to walk free from the bondage of persistent debt.

True Repentance

Repentance begins with a change in the way you think. Then it leads to a change in actions so that earlier offenses are not repeated. It relates to ceasing from sin against God and resolving to obey Him: "I now rejoice, not that you were made sorrowful, but that you were made sorrowful to the point of repentance; for you were made sorrowful according to the will of God, so that you might not suffer loss in anything through us" (2 Corinthians 7:9). Renewal of the mind is critical to repentance. Otherwise, a person will go back to the same old offenses. In order to be free from the old way of life and united with Jesus in a new life, you must have a radical change in thinking. As you renew your mind to the word of God and truly repent, you will be in a position to produce new abundance. "Therefore bear fruit in keeping with repentance" (Matthew 3:8). The fruit of repentance will bring a lasting change.

True Values

The things that are important to carnal people are worthless in God's sight (Luke 16:14-15). Carnal people have a short-term perspective, but God has an eternal perspective. The things of this world will perish, so their value is only temporary. The eternal things that you encounter include spirits and souls of people, fruit of the Spirit, and godly character traits to name just a few. Eternal things have true value from God's perspective. God values family and relationships, as well as the growth and maturity of His family members. Recognizing and acknowledging your position in the royal family of God puts you in a position of authority. Then you can know and fulfill the plan of God for your life. Your faith can become effective. You can rise above the mundane and see what is important from heaven's perspective. Carnal things, such as debt, are destroyed in the presence of the Lord.

True Giving

Believers live through the sacrifice and giving of Jesus Christ. Although Jesus Christ was rich, he became poor so that you might become rich (2 Corinthians 8:9). Follow His example by committing everything to the Lord. Even your life is not your own (1 Corinthians 6:19). He is Lord of everything in your life or Lord of nothing in your life. He could be your Savior without being your Lord. Everything you possess has been given to you by the Lord (1 Corinthians 4:7). He has placed some of His possessions in your hand as a steward over them. When you realize that you are only a steward over His possessions, you can be led by the Holy Spirit in your giving and give from a pure heart. The Lord is more concerned with how you give (the condition of your heart and your motives) than He is with what you give. Jesus said that the widow who offered two small copper coins for the right reasons gave more than those who gave large offerings for the wrong reasons (Mark 12:41-44). He knew things in their hearts were not right. The Lord is looking for purity and purpose in your heart as you give.

True riches are more than material things. The true riches are eternal, and they include salvation, the word of life, the fruit of the Spirit and gifts of the Spirit. True riches are the supernatural abilities, power and strength that believers have with the Lord. The riches of God cannot be corrupted. Abraham had the true riches. He had no lack. Giving the true riches out of purpose and purity is true giving.

Conclusions

Roots live and grow under the surface. Even when not seen, roots can still be growing. Roots of persistent poverty and debt live and grow under the cover of darkness. As long as these roots persist in the lives of people, financial problems will continue to be encountered. Once the roots are identified and brought into the light by the Holy Spirit, they can be destroyed. This chapter has described several roots of poverty and debt and explained how they can be destroyed. Let the Holy Spirit search your heart to see if these roots or any others are keeping you and your family in financial bondage. The roots of poverty and debt have to be destroyed before you and your family can walk in financial freedom.

Chapter 2
KNOWING THE SEASONS

The family of God is entering a new season of prosperity. The Heavenly Father is teaching His children how to prosper and get wealth. Those who have true understanding of His kingdom principles will know how to prosper. They will give and more will come. They will cast their bread on the water, and it will return on every wave (Ecclesiastes 11:1). However, those who hoard and store up for their own pleasure will have the enemy come to corrupt and destroy (Matthew 6:19-20; Luke 12:33).

There are two different approaches to prosperity – the elementary principles of the world versus the principles of the kingdom of God. The kingdom of God is the supernatural realm in which the family of God lives, thrives, matures and operates. It is righteousness, peace and joy in the Holy Spirit (Romans 14:17). There is no room in the kingdom for compromise with worldly principles. While the kingdom stands pure and majestic, the religious system of Christianity has been subjected to deceptive and unfruitful approaches to prosperity. Worldly principles, unfortunately, have been promoted among God's children.

The primary objective of this chapter is to examine kingdom principles of prosperity which relate to the new season. In the past season, worldly principles have been used by God's children. The

Father wants His children to know, however, that the seasons are changing, and this chapter will help explain these changing seasons. The elementary principles of the world will first be explored. Then the major deceptions that were used against God's children in the past season will be identified. Finally, the kingdom principles of prosperity will be examined.

World's System of Prosperity

Prosperity in the world's system focuses on natural things. According to the world, prosperity relates to how much money a person earns and how many things he/she possesses. A person is considered to be prosperous if he/she earns a lot of money with little or no consideration given to expenses, debt or quality of life. People in the world's system use specific elementary principles to guide their lives and actions.

The elementary principles of the world relate to toil, fear and striving for a position of prominence. These principles were first evident at the fall of man in the Garden of Eden, and we can see them still in the world's system of prosperity (Genesis 3:7-19).

Facing lack, Adam and Eve began to toil, or to work extremely hard, for provisions of clothing (verse 7) and food (verse 19). In the world's system, people are expected to toil to meet their own basic necessities and anything else they want.

Facing fear, Adam and Eve sought protection by hiding themselves (verse 8). Guns, houses, investments, insurance and retirement funds are just a few of the instruments used in this world for security and protection.

Facing adversity, Adam and Eve each competed for prominence by trying to put himself/herself in the best possible position. In general, competing for prominence may help people receive more rewards than others when rewards are limited. Likewise, competing for prominence may help people minimize adverse conditions, such as penalties for inappropriate actions. Adam tried to make himself appear better than Eve, claiming that she was responsible for the disobedient act of eating the forbidden fruit (verse 12). Similarly, Eve tried to make herself appear better than the serpent, claiming that the snake was really the one at fault (verse 13). Comparing oneself to others is often used in the world to help improve a person's position.

Hence the elementary principles of the world are toiling for your own provision, providing for your own protection, and striving for prominence because resources in the world are limited. The world's system is based on selfishness. An example of how the application of these principles is clearly seen is when people choose to pursue personal gain by exploiting limited natural resources, such as destruction of endangered species and their habitats, rain forests and coral reefs.

Deceptions in the Old Season

In the old season, the elementary principles of the world were evident among God's children. Flesh, which is the carnal nature of man without divine influence, flourished in the old season. Flesh wants immediate gratification and does not make adequate provision for the future. Flesh wants to keep the old season alive. God's children made provision for the flesh and wanted positions of prominence for themselves and their congregations. Worldly principles have been applied in such a way as to appear spiritual. This approach is like a person standing with his/her feet in two different worlds. Using this approach has brought confusion and unfruitfulness to God's children.

God's children have been subjected to deception in every area of faith, including healing, anointing and righteousness, though the greatest deception has occurred in the area of prosperity. The enemy has stolen more from God's children in the area of prosperity than in any other area. Power is associated with money, and people do unscrupulous things to get money from God's children: "In their greed these [false] teachers will exploit you with stories they have made up" (2 Peter 2:3a). Some major areas of deception that have been evident among Christians will be addressed below.

Appealing to the Carnal Nature but not Stirring the Spirit Man

The soul of man can be manipulated because it is in the carnal realm. But the spirit of man can be moved by the Holy Spirit. Some ministers use carnal appeals to the soul to raise finances for their ministries. Carnal appeals feed the flesh and keep the old season alive. Carnal approaches may produce what appears on the surface to be short-term financial gains for the ministers, but such gains may come at the expense of missing God's favor. Alternatively, anointed ministers can use spiritual approaches to raise finances. Preaching the word of God, informing the people about financial needs and allowing the Holy Spirit freedom to move on the hearts of the people can be elements of a spiritual approach. Both the carnal and spiritual approaches may result in large financial offerings, but there are subtle but important differences between them. The two approaches differ in motives, which are not apparent on the surface. Carnal appeals to the soul are not of God for God is a spirit (John 4:24) and the Father of spirits (Hebrews 12:9). The carnal nature is not subject to God, and those who appeal to carnal appetites do not please God (Romans 8:7-8). Allowing the Holy Spirit to move the hearts of believers is the way God operates. Some examples of carnal appeals are described below to help understand the differences between the two approaches. Your favorite ministry may be doing something similar to one of these examples but may be using a spiritual approach. If so, do not let these simple but real examples offend you.

Feeding hungry children is admirable, but some of the approaches used to solicit support for such ministries reflects carnal motives and so the motives of those ministers raising finances to feed children should be questioned. Carnal ministers often make appeals to the emotions of people in order to raise finances. Showing pictures of hungry children touches people's emotions and purse strings, but using carnal appeals to play on emotions is not of God. Furthermore, if the finances received from these appeals were used for anything other than the feeding of children, the finances were raised using carnal motives.

Blessing and praying for people is admirable, but charging people for these things is not. The motives behind ministers requiring payment in order to bless and pray for people should be questioned. Television ministers frequently offer $1000-blessings and $100-prayers. If viewers send in $1000, they are told to expect to be blessed. Making a promise that people who sent

$1000 would be blessed is a deceptive appeal which caters to the carnal nature. The $1000-blessing is particularly appealing to people controlled by greed. The $1000-blessing is not of God, because the majority of people in the world cannot afford it. God would be a respecter of persons if only rich people could buy a particular blessing, but He does not favor the rich over the poor (Romans 2:11). Similarly, if viewers sent in $100, they were told that the minister would pray for them. If it costs $100 for ministers to pray for people, the people are being robbed. Charging for prayer is carnal and devilish. Is this not making merchandise of the people? Jesus has something to say about this matter. In Matthew 21:12-13 Jesus turned over the moneychangers' tables and cleansed the temple. Then He stated, "My temple will be called a house of prayer, but you have turned it into a den of thieves!"

Sowing financial seed to grow a harvest is admirable, but failure to provide for spiritual growth for God's children is not. Christians have been bombarded with a prominent financial principle – sowing and reaping. Many Christian programs, facilities and ministries have been built on the seed-sowing principle without adequate consideration for maturing God's children. People, needing help with their problems, have been frequently told to sow financial seeds as the remedy. Whether a person's problem was in finances, relationships, or health, the solution frequently appeared to be sowing a financial seed. This approach became a prominent deception in the old season, and biblical principles were used out of context. The proper context would be to address the maturity of the saints. The pure word of

God will result in spiritual growth and, hence, increase (1 Peter 2:2).

In addition, many ministries have relied heavily on the seed-sowing approach to raise funds. However, the approach does not sustain the flow of revenue for these ministries because it does not foster spiritual growth or maturity. When funds in these ministries run low or special projects are planned, additional appeals are made for people to sow more financial seed. Teaching the Word matures people so that they learn to obey the Holy Spirit, especially in their giving. As believers mature spiritually, they will prosper in every area of their lives, including finances. Those ministries that are more concerned about maturing God's children than exploiting them will be abundantly blessed.

The examples given above should be helpful in identifying carnal appeals to the soul. This information should help you avoid those appeals that are obviously not of God. If the appeal caters to emotions or weaknesses, it is not of God. If the appeal lets you buy something of heaven, such as a blessing, that many others in the world could not afford, it is not of God. If the appeal overcharges for products, it is not of God. Such appeals are obviously carnal and easy to avoid. Ministers who use carnal appeals for finances may be spiritual in other areas of their ministry, but carnality can taint or contaminate their overall message. You should always rely on the Holy Spirit within to discern the true motives behind ministers who are asking for your financial support. As a person matures in the Lord, he/she experiences greater spiritual discernment (1 Corinthians 2:14). Carnal people do not have spiritual discernment, but spiritual people grow in discernment. As you exercise your spiritual senses, you will be able to discern the motives of people who are asking for your financial support (Hebrews 5:14). Your spirit will know what is good and what is evil. Stay away from those things that are evil and hold onto those things that are good.

Blessing and cursing are set before you each day (Deuteronomy 30:19-20). Your family will be impacted by whether you choose the blessing or the curse. Which will you choose? If you choose to give because your emotions have been touched, you will not be blessed. Emotional giving is cursed. If you choose to give out of obedience to the Lord, you will be blessed (Isaiah 1:19). Obedient giving is blessed.

Legally Binding but not Life Giving

Another major deception in the area of prosperity relates to keeping believers obligated under the law. Obligation is the lowest form of obedience. Some ministers who preach grace in other areas find it lucrative to preach about finances out of the Old Testament to keep people bound under the law. Legalism comes in all shapes and forms, but the end result is the same – bondage. As the Scriptures tell us, the letter of the law kills, but the Spirit brings life (2 Corinthians 3:6). It is comfortable for the carnal nature to do some things that seem to lead towards righteousness, which is really self-righteousness. For example, the Galatians started a spiritual walk but went back to ritual practices prescribed under the law (Galatians 3:1-3). They were foolish to use human efforts to complete what the Holy Spirit had started in their lives. By reverting to the law described in the Old Testament, they were relying on human efforts rather than on grace.

Adhering to the law of the Old Testament but neglecting Jesus Christ does not ensure an abundant life. A rich young ruler wanted to know God's ways so he asked Jesus how he could receive eternal life (Mark 10:17-22). The young man claimed that he had kept the commandments of God since the time he was a boy. However, he knew something was lacking in his life. He wanted God's life to fill the void in his own life. Keeping the basic commandments did not provide the abundant life that Jesus promised (John 10:10).

Jesus showed the young man how he could have abundant life. He needed to fulfill the Father's plan for his life. He was to sell all that he had, distribute it to the poor, and follow Jesus (Mark 10:21). However, the young man rejected the Father's plan and went away sad, because he wanted to hold on to natural things rather than eternal things. You may have to release the things in your hand in order to receive the things the Father wants to give you. He wants you to have abundant life through Jesus Christ. You receive abundant life by grace through faith, which is the same way you receive salvation.

The Father places riches in the hands of His children so they can learn how to manage them (Luke 16:10-12). If they hold onto the riches as their own possessions, they will be like the young man who rejected the Father's plan for his life. Alternatively, if they realize that their Father owns everything in their hands and that they are merely managers of His affairs, they will do well.

Embracing the Spectacular but Missing the Supernatural

Mass media has provided thrill-a-minute programming to attract audiences. The old thrills did not hold people's attention for long, so more and more thrills were added to keep viewer's attention. The same approach has spread into the religious system to attract and entertain the masses. For example, dynamic productions are used in church services to draw people in. There is more concern about performance than the presence of the Lord. Feel-good messages are preached to soothe the souls of people and keep them coming to services and contributing to the ministries.: "Even from among your own selves men will come to the front who, by saying perverse [distorted and corrupt] things, will endeavor to draw away the disciples after them [to their own party]" (Acts 20:30 AMP). Well-oiled ministry machines are indeed effective in attracting people and their finances; however, people cannot come to Jesus unless the Father draws them by His Spirit (John 6:44). If people are attracted to a ministry for any reason other than the Father's love, word and Holy Spirit, they are not following God.

People rush to ministries that report signs and wonders because they are hungry to experience the spectacular. God is supernatural, but He does grant spectacular signs and wonders to attract unbelievers (1 Corinthians 14:22). It's true that the word of God promises that signs and wonders will follow believers (Mark 16:17-20), but many believers are confused and follow signs and wonders. Signs and wonders from heaven are manifested in the natural realm, so those following such signs and wonders are really only seeking natural things. As long as they are seeking natural things, they can be deceived. When people seek signs and wonders apart from God's order, including character, maturity and accountability in the ministers, they set themselves up for disappointment. As long as people focus on the natural realm the devil can get involved and defeat them. The whirlwind is coming to blow away everything that is of man. Only the things of God will remain.

Religious people are interested in appearances, but real believers walk in the Spirit and sing the praises of Christ (Philippians 3:2-3). Keep your attention on Christ. Let Him have preeminence in your life (Colossians 1:18). Your heart and your mind will be protected if you do this. It is a season of letting go of the things of the past and the things that do not matter and moving into the supernatural. It is time to move into the purpose and into the place that the Lord has for you. The Father desires that His children come into His presence and see His wondrous glory. Looking at carnal things blocks the supernatural. When you put supernatural things above the natural ones, the realm of the eternal becomes available to you (2 Corinthians 4:17-18).

New Season of Kingdom Prosperity

The concept of prosperity in the new season looks inward rather than at outward appearances. Prosperity is changed in the new season to include prosperity in the spirit and soul, as well as in the body or physical and financial realms. Each believer is composed of three parts – spirit, soul, and body. The word of God identifies these three components and declares that all three components can be preserved sound, whole, complete, and blameless: "Now may the God of peace Himself sanctify you entirely; and may your spirit and soul and body be preserved complete, without blame at the coming of our Lord Jesus Christ" (1 Thessalonians 5:23). It is easy to identify the body, which is your head, arms, legs, etc. Your soul, which includes your will, emotions, and mind, is well-known but not visible. Like the soul, the spirit is not visible to the natural eye. The spirit of man is referred to as the hidden person of the heart (1 Peter 3:4), the inner man (Ephesians 3:16), and the innermost being (John 7:38). Hence, the terms of spirit, heart, inner man, and innermost being are used interchangeably.

Kingdom Prosperity Described

The Heavenly Father does not focus on the outward appearance of a person. Instead, He looks deep within a person at the heart and meets him/her there, at the spirit level (1 Samuel 16:7). The Father reveals himself to His children through the heart or spirit of man. If your heart does not condemn you then you are free to receive everything that the Father has promised you (1 John 3:21).

When the Father says a person is poor or rich He is referring to the condition of his/her heart. Here are three passages that support this assertion. First, the rich man described in Luke had so many possessions that he tore down his barns and built larger barns to contain them (Luke 12:16-21). He had an abundance of worldly possessions, but he was a called fool because his soul and spirit were not rich toward God. Second, the believers in Ephesus considered themselves poor because they had few worldly possessions (Revelation 2:9). However, Jesus called them rich because they were rich in the spirit or at the heart level even though they lacked worldly possessions. Third, believers in Laodicea considered themselves rich because they had many worldly possessions (Revelation 3:18). But Jesus said they did not know that they were poor and, in fact, not rich at all. They were poor in spirit, needing to develop their spirits. So we see through these examples that the Father refers to the condition of the heart as being rich or poor, regardless of the amount of worldly possessions. Kingdom prosperity is abundance in the spiritual realm, the mental and emotional realm, and the physical or financial realm.

The Order of Kingdom Prosperity

There is an order to kingdom prosperity: the spirit must first prosper, then the soul prospers, and then the body or physical realm prospers. The spirit is the container and when it overflows from the blessings of heaven it will pour into the soul and onto the body or physical realm.

We see in Scripture that prosperity of the spirit comes first. The very first thing to do is to seek the kingdom of God and His righteousness and then you will have an abundance of all you need: "But seek first His kingdom and His righteousness, and all these things will be added to you" (Matthew 6:33). The kingdom of God and righteousness are spiritual and they build up the spirit man.

Then, the soul has to prosper before you can prosper in the physical or financial realm: "Beloved, I pray that in all respects you may prosper and be in good health, just as your soul prospers" (3 John 1:2). This prayer, which reflects the Father's will, asks that natural prosperity rise to the same level as that of the prosperity of the soul. If the soul prospers at a high level, then the natural prosperity can rise to the same high level. This scripture also implies that prosperity in terms of worldly possessions will not exceed the level of prosperity of the soul. Hence, seek to prosper first in the spirit, second in the soul and then you can prosper in the physical or financial realm. Below are two examples of believers who prospered first in the inner man and then in other aspects of life.

As a young girl, Renee had trouble learning in school. She was placed in special education classes but still showed little aptitude for learning. She eventually dropped out of school without graduating. When we first met Renee, she worked a few hours each week as a crossing guard at a local school and lived in a low-income government housing area. She was raising three children as a single mom, which often caused her to despair over various difficult situations in her life. She came regularly to the services at the mission where we ministered to homeless people. The Holy Spirit imparted abundant life into her. She studied the word of God and committed her life to Jesus. Her journey was often difficult, but the grace and mercy of the Lord changed her life and situation. The Lord did many miraculous things in her life, which would be a story in itself to recount everything. He anointed her with the Holy Spirit and power. She was ordained as a minister by a major denomination and has ministered regularly in church services and with different groups of people. Now Renee works full time and owns a beautiful home. She is an "A" student in college, studying criminal justice to help young people who are in trouble. Her children are successful students, and her oldest child will soon graduate from college. The Lord has done a wonderful work in turning Rene's life around. The change began in her heart, but it has affected every area of her life, including her natural and spiritual families. She is fully committed to the Lord and is giving back to her community.

The Holy Spirit saved, healed and delivered many people through our mission to homeless people, and another example comes from one of those people. One homeless man came to several services, and he always wanted to be near us. Although the man's behavior was peculiar, the Holy Spirit was working in his life. The man went to another city, and we did not see him for several months. Later he returned to give his testimony at our mission. He boldly proclaimed that he had to return to the mission to glorify the Lord. He had been homeless from age 16 to 40. During that time he was never able to have a real job. After the Lord changed his life, he was hired to work in a factory. He was such a good worker that he was promoted to supervisor. He had his own home and had a girlfriend who he planned to marry. He glorified God for changing his life. We saw him a few months later, and he said he was moving into a new home. His family had come from another state to help him move. Let the Lord be glorified for His power to change lives!

Activating Kingdom Principles of Prosperity

Believers have a treasure chest inside, but the treasure chest has to be opened: "The good man brings out of his good treasure what is good" (Matthew 12:35). When the spirit of man is made alive by the Holy Spirit, King Jesus moves inside. He brings with Him the kingdom and all its power and riches. However, all these riches within a believer lie dormant until being activated. In particular, the principles of kingdom prosperity lie dormant inside every believer until activated.

The principles of kingdom prosperity have to be activated in order to benefit the believer and others. Paul instructed Timothy to stir up and set on fire the gift inside him: "For this reason I remind you to kindle afresh the gift of God which is in you through the laying on of my hands" (2 Timothy 1:6-7). The reasons given for stirring up the gift included power, love and discipline or a sound mind (2 Timothy 1:7). You are to be the same: powerful, loving and disciplined with a sound mind. You have the power to produce wealth (Deuteronomy 8:18), the power to give (love) and the discipline and sound mind to know when to produce wealth and when to give.

Only a few of the people around Jesus had love, power and a sound mind. Contrast the woman with the alabaster box of precious ointment and Simon the Pharisee (Luke 7:36-50). The woman loved much and was extravagant in her giving, anointing Jesus with the costly ointment. Jesus had touched the life of this woman, activating the treasure chest within her. The great love inside empowered her to give extravagantly. Simon, however, resented the woman's actions and considered them to be wasteful. Even though he had the means to give, his treasure chest inside had never been activated. He did not love much, so he did not give much. He did not give water or a kiss to Jesus, nor did he anoint Jesus (Luke 7:44-46). Activating the treasure chest inside makes the difference between hoarding up and giving out.

Kingdom principles will be activated through strong relationships with the Godhead – the Father, His Son and His Spirit. The Father is love (1 John 4:8). His Son, Jesus, is the word of God (John 1:1-14). The Holy Spirit is the power of God (Acts 1:8; 10:38). As shown below, loving unconditionally, acting on the word of God and following the Holy Spirit will cause you to be prosperous.

Loving Unconditionally

When the lives of people are truly impacted by the Father's love their treasure chest inside is activated, and they are empowered to give. No longer will they give simply out of obligation or out of fear. No longer will they give grudgingly. Instead, they will joyfully give to fulfill the Lord's purposes. As you joyfully give with a heart filled with love, you will be blessed and you will be a blessing to others.

The distinguishing mark of the new season of prosperity is love. Love gives and keeps on giving! God, who is love, loved the world so much that He gave the best He had – His only begotten Son (John 3:16). Love gives the best. The Heavenly Father's love is unconditional, which means you cannot do anything to earn His love or to lose it. Unconditional love does not seek its own, nor is it selfish (1 Corinthians 13:4-8). Since love is unselfish, it can also be thought of as the power or ability to give.

When you accept Jesus Christ as your Savior you receive the Father's love. The Holy Spirit deposits that love in your heart (Romans 5:5). You receive the Father's love by faith. Love freely releases anything it has. Once you experience unconditional love, you will release and give. You give because the Father's love has been poured into your heart. You no longer give simply out of obligation to satisfy the law and the prophets (Malachi 3:8-12). His love empowers you to give.

People who have not received the love of the Father turn back from following the Lord. People who do not see a need to tithe have not experienced the Father's love. Ministers do not have to pray that people will tithe. Instead, they should pray that the people will have so much love that they will want to give. When you receive His love then you will keep His commandments. Jesus said, "If you love Me, keep My commandments" (John 14:15). The Lord lives with those who love and obey Him. He also reveals Himself to those who love and obey Him (John 14:21). Whenever the Lord reveals Himself to a person, he/she will experience increase. Obedience in loving the Lord and truly loving others will bring prosperity.

Acting on the Word of God

Many people focus on what is happening in the world and what the enemy is doing on the earth. Thoughts about those things are bad seeds that produce nothing but deception. Those thoughts are unprofitable for God's children, causing fear, defeat, poverty, and other evils to manifest. The biggest spiritual deception occurs as people think they are following God when they are really following man. Only the love of the truth will protect people from deception (2 Thessalonians 2:10). Believers are instructed to think on those things that are true and pure rather than on the current events in the world (Philippians 4:8). God's words are the true and pure things to consider.

Let the word of God dwell richly in you and flow out of your mouth (Colossians 3:16). Commit your way unto the Lord, and He will direct your paths (Psalm 37:5; Proverbs 3:6). Be a doer of the word (James 1:22). Those who believe His word and act on His word will prosper. Those who think that the word of God does not apply to them will find themselves outside of the Lord's path.

If the word of God is not preached, people fear and hoard up their money. When the anointed word of God is preached, the local congregation will prosper in every area. The congregation will prosper in finances, in numbers, and in buildings. Most of all, the people will prosper spiritually: being born again, filled with the Spirit, and delivered. If the word of God is preached, any financial yoke will be broken because of the anointing. The anointed word destroys every yoke (Isaiah 10:27). The word has to be preached under the guidance of the Holy Spirit. Those who have been set free by the Son of God, who is also the word of God, are free to give and free to receive (John 8:36). Both giving and receiving are involved in deliverance and prosperity. Faith comes from the word of God (Romans 10:17). As you receive more revealed word, your faith grows. Have faith, for only with faith can you please the Lord (Hebrews 11:6). Live in faith, speak in faith and move in faith.

Following the Holy Spirit

If the word is not preached with the Spirit's anointing, the people are not clean. They are tainted by the world, and their actions are tainted by the world. The Holy Spirit cleanses and sanctifies believers (1 Corinthians 6:11). The world hoards up, but the spirit man who is led by the Holy Spirit freely gives. Freely you have received so freely give is a spiritual principle (Matthew 10:8). When a person's life has been touched by the Lord, he freely gives of himself, his material possessions, and his praise. The lame man at the Gate Beautiful was healed and then moved into action (Acts 3:1-10). Peter and John gave what they had – the anointing which rested on the word. They gave it to that man, and it freed him and energized him. Then he freely gave. He went into the temple, leaping and praising God.

Be filled with the Holy Spirit and rejoice in what the Lord is doing (Ephesians 5:18). Carnality is being exposed, and flesh is being cut away. Only those who are comforted by the Holy Spirit can stand in this day. Those who hear the Holy Spirit and obey Him will be comforted, will find peace in tribulation and will begin to grow and get strong. Those are the ones the Lord will use to bridge the gap for those in trouble so they can reach the Lord. They will preach the gospel to those who hunger and thirst after righteousness. They will pull to safety those who have fallen into holes. Listen to the Holy Spirit and you will prosper. Follow the Holy Spirit and your every need and every want will be met by the Lord. The more the Holy Spirit is allowed to move and to flow through you the more you will increase.

Conclusions

There has been a shift in the seasons. The carnal principles that appeared to work in the past will not work in the new season for these are perilous times. The era of widespread prosperity that the world experienced in the past has gone and will not return. Some may experience a form of prosperity for a time, but increasing turmoil will be experienced by the multitudes. In the dark days that lay ahead for the world, believers will be turning to the Lord and His ways. They will find the abundance that they are seeking only under His sheltering arms.

Do not focus on times past, but focus on the new and bright dawn that is coming forth for the people who love the Lord Jesus. He is the bright and morning star (Revelation 22:16). Let His light shine (John 9:5) because it radiates His everlasting love. Let it saturate you and make you full. Let it penetrate the hearts of others.

It is the season for believers to demonstrate the Father's love in their own lives and to share His love with others. You can demonstrate the Father's love to others only to the extent to which it has been deposited in you. His love will be poured out in its fullness in the last days to restore and prepare the family of God for its intended purpose.

Chapter 3

THE FATHER'S FOUNDATION FOR PROSPERITY

The Father had a great kingdom, but He wanted a family. Love motivated Him to venture His entire kingdom for family. He made a promise to Abraham to birth a family, and He swore an oath by Himself to confirm it (Hebrews 6:13-14). The oath staked His entire being on fulfilling the promise of family. His plan was flawless and the great goal of family is being realized. The family of God, which is the fulfillment of the promise, is realized in Christ and His body (Galatians 3:29).

The Father's kingdom is advancing and will supersede all other kingdoms of this world (Revelation 11:15). To further this process of advancing the kingdom, Jesus taught the disciples to pray that the Father's kingdom come (Luke 11:2). All things in the Father's kingdom are available to those who seek it (Matthew 6:33). The Father has bestowed all spiritual blessings on His family through their union with His Son, Jesus Christ (Ephesians 1:3). Even though prosperity is available for believers, many have been deceived by thinking that they can prosper just by following specific steps. Instead, prosperity comes from a believer's relationship with the Father, His Son and His Spirit.

The Father is the core of His kingdom and the prosperity that flows out of His kingdom. The foundational concepts for kingdom prosperity relate directly to the Father Himself. The foundation for the family of God and hence kingdom prosperity is laid by apostles and prophets on His Son, Jesus Christ who is the cornerstone (Ephesians 2:19-20). The first foundation is love, for the Father is love (1 John 4:8). This first foundation has already been addressed in the preceding chapter of this book; this current chapter deals with three other foundational concepts – contentment, purity, and righteousness. The common thread linking these foundational concepts is "with the Father."

- Contentment denotes a close relationship with the Father.
- Purity denotes walking consistently with the Father.
- Righteousness denotes being in the proper position with the Father.

Operating in these foundational concepts will help bring kingdom prosperity to the family of God. This chapter examines contentment, purity and righteousness and shows how they relate to kingdom prosperity.

Contentment

While the writings of King David showed the process of reverencing the Lord, his son Solomon revealed the end result. The entire book of the Song of Solomon is a love story between the lover and his beloved (Song of Solomon 1:8). It reveals a loving relationship between the Lord and the believer. The lover and the beloved are deeply in love with each other and want to spend intimate time together. A key to the love story is contentment. The beloved brought contentment to her lover: "Thus I have become in his eyes like one bringing contentment (Song of Solomon 8:10b, NIV). She was in love and content, and the lover felt contentment in her presence as well. Wherever the lover went he remembered the contentment that he felt only in the presence of his beloved. He could not wait to return to her.

As a believer, you can have this same love affair with the Lord. Your contentment comes from a strong relationship with Him (Hebrews 13:5). He wants you to be like the beloved in the Song of Solomon and bring contentment. He says, "Bring Me contentment!" As you bring contentment into the love affair, you touch the Lord, for He is easily touched (Hebrews 4:15). As you bring contentment, the Lord is content being with you. As you truly experience His love you can impart love to others, impacting their lives.

Contentment comes from having a relationship with the heavenly Father. Believers can be content, knowing that the Lord is with them: "Make sure that your character is free from the love of money, being content with what you have; for He Himself has said, 'I will never desert you, nor will I ever forsake you'" (Hebrews 13:5). Contentment is based on your relationship with the Lord rather than on the things which you possess.

There are varying degrees of contentment depending on your relationship with the Father. The more you trust Him, the greater your contentment will be. In Psalm 23 David reached a place of contentment. The contentment David expressed in this passage was derived from his relationship with the Lord as his shepherd.

Likewise, Paul, in Philippians, did not look at his situation, but he reminded himself that he could trust the Father to take care of him. He said, "Not that I speak from want, for I have learned to be content in whatever circumstances I am in" (Philippians 4:11). He was content while experiencing weakness, insults, distress, persecutions, and difficulties (1 Corinthians 12:10).

You can be content without being complacent. You can be content without being satisfied where you are. Contentment is not satisfaction, but it is your relationship and trust in the Lord. Being satisfied or not satisfied is not contentment. Contentment is a spiritual word that has nothing to do with circumstances or what you possess or what you do not possess.

Your relationship with the Father cannot be based on what He can give you or what you can do for Him. Your relationship with Him must be based on who He is. People followed Jesus for many different reasons. Many followed Him for the miracles which He performed (John 6:2). Those people were looking for the things they could get from him, such as healing, fish and loaves of bread. Some of His followers were caught up in serving Him. Martha was distracted, worried and bothered with all her serving (Luke 10:40-41). But Mary just wanted to be close to Jesus. She chose to sit at His feet and hear His words (Luke 10:42). You are to follow Mary's example of a close relationship.

Your relationship with the Father determines your relationship with others. Since God is love (1 John 4:8), the more time you spend with Him, the more of His love you receive. As you receive His love, then you will have love to pour out on others.

There are those who have gone back from serving the Lord, seeking something other than the kingdom of God. Peter and several of the other disciples went back to fishing after the death and resurrection of Jesus (John 21:2-3). Those who go back may get what they want, but they will not experience contentment outside of a vibrant relationship with the Father.

Your life does not consist of what you have or what you do for others. Your life consists of how well you know the Father, the Son, and the Holy Spirit. As we read in John 17:3, "This is eternal life, that they may know You, the only true God, and Jesus Christ whom You have sent." Out of knowing the Lord, doors will open up to impact others. Go for the impact!

Purity

Keep yourself pure (1 Timothy 5:22). Purity denotes walking with the Father. The Father is pure and cannot stand the sight of evil (Habakkuk 1:13). All those who hope to see the Father purify themselves just as the Father and the Son are pure (1 John 3:3). The cleansing comes from accepting the work of the cross on which Jesus shed His blood and died. Only those with a pure heart can stand in the presence of the Father (Psalm 24:3-4). Only those with a pure heart can see Him (Matthew 5:8). Seeing or perceiving the Father is spiritual. You see the Father with your spiritual eyes and not your natural eyes. An effective relationship with the Father requires your seeing Him through your spiritual eyes and spiritual understanding.

The Father is a spirit (John 4:24) and the Father of spirits (Hebrews 12:9). Those who walk with Him must walk in spirit and truth (John 4:23; Romans 8:1). Walking in the spirit involves submitting to the Father's will (Hebrews 12:9), being led by His Spirit (Romans 8:14) and reflecting the nature of Christ (2 Corinthians 5:20).

It is important to purify your heart before giving an offering or doing anything for the Lord. Your heart has to be pure in order for your offering to be acceptable to Him (Matthew 5:23-24 and 6:1-2) You are to be reconciled with others before offering a gift to the Lord. Holding unforgiveness, bitterness or anger in a person's heart keeps the offering from being acceptable to the Lord. A person may receive recognition from men for giving a large offering out of impure motives, but the Lord looks on the heart. People cannot count on a reward from the Lord with iniquities or impurities in their heart even though they give a big offering. The churches of Macedonia are a great example of giving out of a pure heart, because they first gave themselves to the Lord before they offered their gifts to Him (2 Corinthians 8:5).

All impurities in your heart must be removed in order to have a vibrant relationship with the Father and walk closely with Him. It is time to go down to the river that ushers out from His throne (Psalm 46:4; Revelation 22:1). Go down to the river and submerge yourself in the water of the anointed word and the Holy Spirit (Ephesians 5:26). Go down to the river so that you might be cleansed. Put your whole self into the river and you will see none of yourself and only the Lord. It is a pure river that washes you (Revelation 22:1). The river has healing and cleansing in it (Ezekiel 47:9). You will be strengthened. Do not be weary in well doing (Galatians 6:9), but come to the river of life.

Considering the anointed word of God and the Holy Spirit as a mighty river is helpful for two reasons. First, the concept of the river connects you to its source, which is your Father's throne. He reigns from His throne. Your praises establish His throne in your heart (Psalm 22:3). Second, the river brings life, abundance and prosperity wherever it freely flows. Without the river, the land (or your life) would be barren and desolate. There is no end to the flow of this mighty river through all situations and all seasons of life.

If the garden of your heart is well watered by the river of life, you will bring forth much fruit. The fruit of the Spirit that can be brought forth in your heart includes love, joy and peace. Unconditional love governs everything that is done in the Father's kingdom (2 Corinthians 5:14; James 2:8). Along with love, which is one of the foundations already discussed in this book, joy and peace are major components of His kingdom (Romans 14:17). A well watered and fruitful garden is a pleasant place for you to walk with your Father. Like Adam walked with the Lord in the garden in the cool of the day (Genesis 3:8), you will be able to walk with your Father. You will be able to share your heart with Him and to know His heart, experiencing the abundant life (John 17:3; John 10:10).

Righteousness

The first priority for believers is to seek the kingdom of God and His righteousness (Matthew 6:33). Righteousness means right standing with God. You become the righteousness of God in Jesus Christ. 2 Corinthians says, "God made him who had no sin to be sin for us, so that in him we might become the righteousness of God" (2 Corinthians 5:21). Righteousness relates to being right with the Father rather than doing the right things. However, doing the right things flows out of being right with the Father. The one who practices righteousness is righteous (1 John 3:7). Be workers of righteousness and hold fast to what is pure.

Righteousness denotes proper position with the Father. Through Christ Jesus you have access into the proper position, which is the throne room of God (Hebrews 4:16). Believers are now seated at the right hand of Jesus: "And [God] raised us up with Him, and seated us with Him in the heavenly places in Christ Jesus" (Ephesians 2:6). The Lord is a refuge for the righteous (Psalm 64:10). A refuge is a place of safety where people can learn about the word of God. The Father wants His children to know His ways. David wanted to know the ways of the Lord (Psalm 25:4). His ways are made known in His sanctuary (Psalm 77:13). His sanctuary is not in buildings made with hands, but it is in the inner man (2 Corinthians 6:16). The Father's ways are known in your inner man.

It takes the energy of the Holy Spirit flowing through believers in order for them to take their rightful position in the body of Christ. As we read in 1 Corinthians 12:13, "For by one Spirit we were all baptized into one body, whether Jews or Greeks, whether slaves or free, and we were all made to drink of one Spirit." Your rightful position in the body of Christ is a place where your inner man can be awakened. It is a place where the kingdom of God is being enlarged and expanded within you. True ministers will awaken the people unto righteousness and unto holiness and prepare them for purpose. If you hunger and thirst for righteousness you will be filled (Matthew 5:6).

Some people are out of position because they have gone ahead of the Lord, not knowing His ways or His thoughts (Isaiah 55:9). Knowing the Lord makes you strong and able to withstand the winds of change. Below is an example of how being out of position blocks prosperity and how getting into the right position attracts prosperity.

A young man who came to the services at the mission started his own business. His mother borrowed some money to help him get started. His business generated a lot of income, but he borrowed to buy additional equipment, pay expenses, buy a new home, etc. He was not able to pay off his debt. Sherry counseled him, advising him to pay off what his mother had borrowed for him. He paid his mother's debt, which was the righteous thing to do. After he cleared up the situation with his mother, he was able to pay off several other creditors. A person cannot prosper when things are out of order. When things are put in order, a person is in a position to prosper.

You will not fail if you are in the right position. Have faith in the Lord and He will lead you in the paths of righteousness. You can follow the path of righteousness for His word will lead you, guide you, and promote you. As you advance along the path of righteousness, the enemy cannot stand before you.

The biblical analogy of trees of righteousness can help illuminate the concept of righteousness. The Lord has planted His people as trees of righteousness (Isaiah 61:3). You are a tree of righteousness on the basis of your relationship with the Lord. Knowing the Lord extends and strengthens your root system.

When your roots are strong they go deep into the water of His word and Spirit. You can receive nourishment and strength from the word of God. For example, as the fig tree begins to bloom, you know that its fruit is coming. You are like that fig tree, blooming in the sight of the Lord, as the Scripture says: "You did not choose Me but I chose you, and appointed you that you would go and bear fruit, and that your fruit would remain, so that whatever you ask of the Father in My name He may give to you" (John 15:16). Soon He will come to inspect the fruit. He will taste it to see that it is good.

There are many advantages of knowing that you are the righteousness of God in Christ Jesus. When you are the righteousness of God, you have access to the throne of God where you can obtain help, grace and mercy (Hebrews 4:16). Your earnest prayers are powerful (James 5:16). Your Father responds as requested because you are His child. He gives only good gifts to His children (Luke 11:13).

Balance

Believers will prosper when they are content, pure in their hearts and when they know their position in the Father. By looking at David in the Psalms, you can see when he operated in contentment, purity and righteousness. You can see when David's authority increased and when it decreased. David's authority increased when he was close to the Lord, following His ways. When David had Uriah murdered and subsequently took his wife for himself, he was impure and lost authority in the spiritual realm (2 Samuel 12:9). If a person is content and walking with the Father and is in the right position, he has great authority. If one of these foundations is missing then a person's authority in the spiritual realm is diminished. These three words – contentment, purity and righteousness – are spiritual words that have nothing to do with the natural realm.

The enemy has a plan against the people of God to destroy the foundation on which their lives are built. The enemy's plan is to:

• Interrupt relationship building between the child and the Father
• Get a person involved in impure and immoral lifestyles, thoughts and actions
• Move a person out of position of right standing with the Father

If the foundation is destroyed, nothing else in a person's life will stand. Then the enemy can steal, kill and destroy purpose and destiny (John 10:10).

Be cautious of your words for they bring life or death (Proverbs 18:21). If a person speaks the Word of God then those words will bring life and freedom. When the Spirit of Life takes hold of your tongue, He brings liberty. He brings contentment, purity and righteousness. When people do not have these three things balanced in their lives, there will be an imbalance and they will be tossed to and fro. When people operate in contentment, purity and righteousness, they are not easily deceived or moved by this natural realm. Jesus was not moved by questions or actions of Pharisees, not moved by Legion, not moved by men's plans to stone a woman, and not moved by the cross. In other words, He was not moved by circumstance. When these foundations are established in your life you, too, can stand firm on the rock, Christ Jesus, against all earthly circumstances.

Conclusions

Many new revelations on prosperity are being expounded in these days. They may sound good on the surface, but if they are not built on a biblical foundation they will not witness with your spirit man. Any revelation that is not built on the Father's firm foundation will fail. Are you building your life on the firm foundation that will help you enter into the abundant life that Jesus died to give you? Chapters 2 and 3 presented foundational truths for prosperity. A personal relationship with Jesus as your Savior and Lord is the cornerstone of the foundation (Ephesians 2:20). Faith and authority flow from your relationship with Jesus. A personal relationship with the Holy Spirit will provide guidance for a supernatural life in which you will be able to draw on the Father's abundance. A personal relationship with the Father, who is love, will change your thoughts and motives to be more like Him and supernaturally energize your faith. Strong personal relationships with the Father, His Spirit and His Son will radically change your life and cause you and your family to prosper.

Chapter 4

THE KINGDOM SPIRIT

When people travel to various regions or countries, they may notice different attitudes or perspectives. For example, a spirit of industry and optimism may be evident in one region, while a spirit of poverty and oppression may be evident in another. Similarly, believers who operate effectively in the kingdom of God demonstrate a different attitude and perspective than those whose focus is on the natural realm. Those who walk in the kingdom are said to have a kingdom spirit.

Jesus taught that only one specific spirit receives the kingdom: "Blessed are the poor in spirit, for theirs is the kingdom of heaven" (Matthew 5:3). This verse refers to the spirit of man rather than the Holy Spirit. The translation of this verse in the *Amplified Bible* describes this spirit as the humble, who rate themselves insignificant. The *Amplified Bible* also says God's favor is on this spirit. *Young's Literal Translation* states that a person with this spirit will reign in the heavens. For the purposes of this study, this spirit will be called the kingdom spirit or the spirit of the kingdom. Even though Jesus did not elaborate on the kingdom spirit in this verse, the concept of the kingdom spirit is clearly explained in the word of God. The kingdom spirit is defined as the Spirit of God manifested in human flesh: "And the Word became flesh, and dwelt among us, and we saw His glory, glory as of the only begotten from the Father, full of grace and truth" (John 1:14). Jesus taught that His words are spirit and life (John 6:63). He is called Immanuel, which means, "God with us" (Matthew 1:23).

The kingdom spirit is formidable and fearless, always following the Lord at any cost. This spirit is filled with heaven's wisdom and might. It is a vessel of anointing and power to proclaim the gospel of the kingdom and to set the captives free. The kingdom spirit ministers to the King by feeding the hungry, healing the sick and visiting orphans and widows. The kingdom spirit is favored by God and man.

The kingdom spirit manifests the fruit of the Spirit, including love, joy and peace (Galatians 5:22-23). It would be expected to operate in the gifts of the Spirit such as faith, words of wisdom and prophecies (1 Corinthians 12:8-10). It gives a visible form to the spirit of wisdom and revelation (Ephesians 1:17) and the spirit of faith (2 Corinthians 4:13).

This chapter examines the kingdom spirit. It shows how the Spirit of God working through a person can bring him/her out of obscurity to a position of authority and to prosper greatly. It shows how to develop a kingdom spirit and how to operate in a kingdom spirit.

Reigning over Foreign Kingdoms

The word of God describes the lives of many men and women who rose out of obscurity to prominent positions of power and influence. This section will consider three of God's people who rose out of obscurity to reign over foreign kingdoms because they were rich toward God. Two of the three, Joseph and Daniel, were carried as captives away from their homeland into foreign nations, but they rose out of obscurity to rule over those nations. Joseph was a ruler in Egypt. Daniel was a ruler in both the Babylonian and Persian Empires. The third, Esther, who was a member of the conquered Jewish nation in a foreign country, rose from obscurity to reign as queen of the Persian Empire. These three Hebrews (meaning those from the other side) had no wealth, no connection with influential people, and no other natural reason to be promoted to a position of great authority. It was only their relationship with the Lord and His favor upon them that brought them to positions of influence. They used their positions and influence in foreign kingdoms to protect, sustain and provide for God's people.

Joseph's Promotion to Ruler

Joseph saw himself as a ruler long before he was promoted to a position of great authority. Through dreams the Lord imparted life and destiny into Joseph while he was a teenager. His two dreams indicated that he would be a person with authority (Genesis 37:5-11). His brothers were jealous and hated him, and his father rebuked him for the dreams. Joseph's brothers sold him into slavery in Egypt as their way of stopping the dreams from being fulfilled (Genesis 37:28). Nevertheless, the dreams were from the Lord and would come to pass. While Joseph remained in slavery and later in prison, the Lord was with him and caused him to prosper (Genesis 39:2-3; 21-23). Joseph was a diligent worker with integrity and other godly character traits, so he was quickly promoted in every situation (Genesis 39:4; 22-23). It was Joseph's ability to interpret dreams that gave him an audience with Pharaoh (Genesis 40:8-14). Pharaoh dreamed two dreams that could not be interpreted by any of his servants. When Joseph interpreted his dreams, Pharaoh recognized that Joseph was discerning, wise, and filled with the Spirit of God (Genesis 41:38-39). Therefore, Pharaoh made Joseph ruler over the people of Egypt with the responsibility to store grain when harvests were plentiful and then distribute grain during famine (Genesis 41:40). Joseph's brothers came to Egypt for grain and bowed before Joseph as his dreams foretold. Even though Joseph was in a position to take revenge on his brothers for the way they treated him, he forgave them and treated them well.

Joseph was responsible for relocating his father, Israel, and his extended family to Egypt. He sustained them during a severe famine. Joseph and his 11 brothers became progenitors of the twelve tribes of Israel, which the Lord later brought out of Egypt as a nation. Hence, Joseph played an important role in the early history of the nation of Israel.

Esther's Promotion to Ruler

Esther was a beautiful young Jewish woman in the Persian Empire, where her people had been relocated after being conquered (Esther 2-9). Esther was prepared for several months to appear before the king. The king loved Esther and chose her to be queen. Even as queen, Esther remained obedient to Mordecai, who raised her after her parents died. An influential prince in Babylon planned to kill Mordecai and destroy all the Jews. When Esther was informed about this plan to destroy her people and her, she called for a fast to prepare her to seek the Lord. The Lord gave her wisdom to overcome the enemy. Her wisdom was evident as she developed a clever plan to ask the king for help against the enemy of the Jews. She risked her own life to appear before the king without being summoned. Before going to the king she made this courageous statement: "If I perish, I perish" (Esther 4:16). She found favor in the sight of the king, and he offered to grant her petition to half of his kingdom. Delivering her people was more important to Esther than the king's offer of half the kingdom. When Esther's plan unfolded, the king destroyed her enemy and gave his wealth to her. Consequently, her people were able to defend themselves and defeat their enemies. Esther became influential in the Persian Empire. Hence, Esther played an important historical role in sustaining the nation of Israel, which was predominantly the Jews which she protected.

Daniel's Promotion to Ruler

Daniel and three other young men were chosen from the captured Israelite nobility and prepared to serve the king of Babylon (Daniel 1-2). They were chosen for their wisdom, knowledge and understanding. Daniel purposed in his heart to eat only those foods approved by the Lord. The Lord gave these four young men an unusual aptitude for learning. He gave Daniel the ability to understand visions and dreams. The king had a dream and asked for someone to interpret it. Daniel prayed with the other Hebrew young men for an interpretation of the dream. God revealed the dream and its interpretation to Daniel. The dream described a succession of kingdoms from Babylon to the present. The final kingdom was the kingdom of heaven, which will reign forever.

Then Daniel thanked God and praised Him for the interpretation, wisdom and might. When he interpreted the dream for the king, the king made him ruler over Babylon (Daniel 2:47-48).

Daniel continued to be influential in the court of several rulers, including the Persian conquerors. By studying the word of God, he knew when it was time for the fulfillment of Jeremiah's prophecy for the return of the people of Israel to their homeland (Jeremiah 25:11; Daniel 9:1-19). He prayed for this prophecy to be fulfilled. Then, as a member of the royal court in the Persian Empire, Daniel was influential in returning the people of Israel to their homeland (Ezra 1:1-4).

Common Threads

Even with humble beginnings, these three Hebrews saw themselves as rulers. They demonstrated a kingdom spirit while in difficult situations. Joseph had a divine spirit (Genesis 41:39). Esther portrayed the new spirit under the control of the Holy Spirit. Daniel had an excellent spirit (Daniel 6:3). They rose from obscurity to rule in foreign kingdoms. However, their highest priority was to serve the Lord, while caring for His people and advancing His kingdom. They played important roles in sustaining and protecting God's people. Joseph sustained Israel in the early stages of the nation. Esther protected the Jewish nation while in captivity. Daniel was instrumental in returning the people of Israel to their homeland.

Joseph, Esther, and Daniel knew the Lord. Each of these three Hebrews had a close personal relationship with Him. They fasted and prayed, seeking the Lord's will and help. The Lord deposited wisdom and power in them. The Lord was with Joseph in slavery and in prison and gave him the interpretation of dreams (Genesis 39:2, 21). Pharaoh recognized that the Spirit of God was with Joseph (Genesis 41:38). Esther called a fast to seek the Lord before going on a perilous mission to deliver her people (Esther 4:16). Daniel openly prayed and gave thanks and continually served the Lord (Daniel 6:10, 16).

The favor of the Lord was on these three Hebrews. The Lord's favor on a person causes others to favor them, as well. The favor of the Lord and man is upon those people who live by the truth and show mercy and kindness (Proverbs 3:3-4). They will also be highly esteemed by the Lord and man. Joseph's father favored him above his brothers and gave him a beautiful robe (Genesis 37:3). All three were favored by their handlers in the foreign lands. The Lord gave Joseph favor with the official who was in charge of the prison (Genesis 39:21). The Lord gave Esther favor with the official in charge of the women in the king's palace (Esther 2:8-9). The Lord gave Daniel favor with the official in charge of his training (Daniel 1:9). Having favor with the initial handlers gave these Hebrews access to kings. Having the Lord's favor on their lives caused the kings to give them favor and promote them to positions of great authority. You do not need favor with everyone. You may only need favor with those in a position to give you access to those in key positions.

These three Hebrews showed that they were fearless in the face of adversity. Joseph risked being thrown into prison rather than give up his integrity (Genesis 39:7-20). Esther risked death to deliver her people from destruction (Esther 4:11). Daniel risked being thrown into the lions' den and death in order to serve the Lord (Daniel 6:12-16).

These three Hebrews knew when the seasons were changing. Joseph knew when to store grain and when to distribute grain (Genesis 41:34-36). Esther knew when to diligently pursue deliverance for her people (Esther 4:16-17; 5:1-3). Daniel knew when it was time for the people of Israel to be returned to their homeland (Daniel 9:1-19). Believers need to know when the seasons are changing. A kingdom spirit will help you recognize when the seasons are changing.

Practical Application

As a young man, I came out of nowhere to a position of authority in the secular realm because of my kingdom spirit. I gave the Lord first place in my life and professional career. The favor of the Lord and man was upon me. I held a position as Distinguished Professor of Applied Economics at a major university. I won numerous research and teaching awards, including a creative research medal. I was content in research and teaching, but the Holy Spirit directed me to apply for an administrative position at the university. The Holy Spirit assured me that I would be selected for the position. The position was initially offered to someone else, but I knew the position belonged to me. The other person negotiated with the university but finally took an offer elsewhere, and the position was then offered to me. The earlier negotiations by the other person benefitted me, as he was able to negotiate a better offer than otherwise possible. I found favor with upper administrators to be selected and then to serve as an administrator. When I first began to serve in that role, Sherry gave my unit a prophetic word that there would be seven years of prosperity under my administration. It was a prosperous period with many of the programs being recognized for excellence. As an administrator, I continued to seek the Lord in carrying out my responsibilities. I was persecuted and threatened over many issues, but I sought to do those things that were right in the sight of the Lord. I made many contributions to the programs of my unit, including hiring and promoting many good people. Through the prophetic word, I knew when the seasons were changing and when to relinquish my position as an administrator. While I was a university administrator, I was actively involved in ministry to the homeless and oppressed, including those in jails and prisons. I also traveled widely internationally, ministering in many countries.

Reigning in God's Spiritual Kingdom

The kingdom of God represents the Heavenly Father's business. The word of God uses numerous analogies to show that the Father is in the olive and grape business. The oil from the olives represents the anointing (Mark 6:13; Hebrews 1:9; James 5:14). The wine from the grapes represents the power of the Holy Spirit (Acts 2:15-18; Ephesians 5:18). When Jesus reached the age of accountability, He joined the Father's business as an apprentice (Luke 2:49). Jesus spent several years being fully immersed in the Father's oil (anointing) and wine (power). He increased in wisdom and in favor with God and men (Luke 2:52). He learned how to be the Father's representative or ambassador. Jesus became the exact expression of the Father on the earth (Hebrews 1:3). He only spoke what He heard the Father say (John 8:26). He only did what He saw the Father do (John 5:19). In His first public address, Jesus proclaimed that the Spirit of the Lord had anointed Him to preach, heal and set the captives free (Luke 4:16-19). The Father anointed Jesus with the Holy Ghost and power to do good and heal the oppressed (Acts 10:38).

Jesus demonstrated the kingdom spirit. He taught about the kingdom and did the work of the kingdom. In the book of Matthew alone, Jesus referred to the kingdom over 50 times: Jesus was going through all the cities and villages, teaching in their synagogues and proclaiming the gospel of the kingdom and healing every kind of disease and every kind of sickness" (Matthew 9:35). Jesus truly sought the kingdom of God above everything else. He commanded believers to seek the kingdom first (Matthew 6:33). He formed all believers into a kingdom, or royal race (Revelation 1:6). The book of Revelation shows that Jesus will continue to work in the vineyard, treading out the grapes in the Father's winepress (Revelation 19:15).

In the book of Matthew, Jesus teaches 12 parables about the kingdom. Four of His parables on the kingdom in Matthew 13 refer to inanimate objects – seed, leaven, treasure and a net. The other eight parables of the kingdom refer to people. One person sought treasure (Matthew 13:45) and another owned treasure (Matthew 13:52). One person sowed seed in his field (Matthew 13:24) and another hired laborers for his vineyard (Matthew 20:1). One person gave oversight of his resources to his servants (Matthew 25:14), and another settled accounts with his servants (Matthew 18:23). One person made a marriage for his son

(Matthew 22:2). In one parable, five virgins had oil for their lamps and five others looked for oil (Matthew 25:1).

The owner of a vineyard typifies the kingdom. Jesus taught several parables about the kingdom that relate to a householder, or head of an extended family, who owned a vineyard (Matthew 20:1-16; Mark 12:1-8). The householder planted the vineyard, he built a wall, a winepress and a watchtower, and then he turned the property over to stewards (vine-dressers and husbandmen) who would care for it (Mark 12:1). He sent several servants to the stewards to receive his share of the harvest. However, the stewards mistreated the servants and refused to pay them. Then the owner of the vineyard sent his son to the stewards, expecting that they would honor him (Mark 12:6). Although the evil stewards in the parable rejected the son, good stewards today can accept the Son of God, Jesus. The story of the vineyard continues to unfold throughout the word of God to explain the kingdom. This story of the vineyard relates to every believer.

God's children are described as branches on the vine (John 15:5) and the olive tree (Romans 11:17). As stewards in the vineyard and the olive garden, believers have a responsibility to care for the Father's children. Jesus taught that the harvest is plentiful, but there are few laborers, or stewards, working in the harvest (Matthew 9:37-38). He instructed believers to pray that the Father would send more laborers into the harvest. It is important to recognize that you have been called as a steward in the Father's business. Let the attitude of a good steward in the Father's business influence your life and the decisions that you make.

Here is a story that helps explain how believers can operate in the Father's olive and grape business. The Good Samaritan found a half-dead, naked Jew on a road from Jerusalem to Jericho (Luke 10:30-35). The young Jew was traveling on the road when robbers attacked him. They wounded him and left him for dead. Although the religious people who passed by offered no help to the wounded man, the Samaritan aided him. He poured oil and wine into his wounds and then brought him to the safety of an inn. Believers can operate the same way, helping others who are wounded spiritually, emotionally and/or physically and who need the oil and wine from the Lord. He has anointed believers with the Holy Ghost and the power to help those in need.

Sherry truly has a kingdom spirit. She believes that if the Holy Spirit knows something, she can find it out because of her close relationship with Him. She prays for people to be healed and delivered everywhere she goes. Many people have testified later that they were healed or delivered through her prayers. She has a special anointing to pray for barren women to conceive and have children. Sherry waited through 14 years of marriage before giving birth to a child, so she comforts others with the same comfort that the Lord poured into her life. Many women have called or told her about how the Lord blessed them with children after she prayed for them. Recently, a salesperson in a department store stopped Sherry to report that she has three children as a result of Sherry's prayers. A few years earlier, Sherry heard the woman tell someone in the store that she was unable to have children. Sherry stopped and asked if she could pray for the woman to have children. She was able to pray with the woman, and the saleswoman became pregnant soon afterwards and did not have any other trouble conceiving. Praise the Lord for His great mercy!

Prospering the King

The distinguishing mark of the kingdom spirit is prospering the king. The person with a kingdom spirit will put the king's interests above his/her own interests. When people prosper the king, they will prosper.

Joseph, Esther and Daniel prospered the kings who ruled over them. The kings had confidence that these Hebrews would make sure that everything was in order (Daniel 6:2 The Message). The kings would not suffer loss or damage, because these Hebrews would look after their interests. The kings gave these Hebrews their own rings, robes and other gifts, as well as authority over their kingdoms (Genesis 41:42; Esther 8:7-8; Daniel 3:48).

Jesus has all authority in heaven and earth, which makes Him the King (Matthew 28:18). He is the King of Kings and Lord of Lords (Revelation 17:14 and 19:16). When believers prosper King Jesus, then they will prosper. How do you prosper the King? Make Him your first priority. Magnify Him in every situation. Praise and worship Him for He is worthy of all praise.

Here are several practical ways to prosper King Jesus. First, believe King Jesus. Let His word be the truth and let everything that is contrary to His word be considered a lie (Romans 3:4). If Jesus says you are prosperous and the world says you are poor, who will you believe? Again, believe Jesus. All things are possible to those who believe (Mark 9:23). Second, obey the King. Be sensitive to His Spirit and quick to obey His commands.

Obedience brings prosperity. The great commission is to teach others to obey the King (Matthew 28:19-20). Third, walk in peace. Jesus overcame the world, defeated the enemy and gave His peace to believers (John 16:33; 1 John 3:8). Now believers are to maintain the peace that Jesus purchased (Philippians 4:7). Pray for the peace of Jerusalem and His church, which Jerusalem symbolizes, so that you will prosper (Psalm 122:6). Fourth, fulfill your purpose and destiny. Each believer is destined to be conformed to the image of Jesus Christ (Romans 8:29). In addition, there is a specific purpose for each person on this earth. Fulfill the purpose which only you can fulfill.

Another important way to prosper King Jesus is to show Him compassion. The first verse in Psalm 18 is generally translated, "I will love the Lord." However, it could literally be translated, "I will have compassion on the Lord." The Hebrew word translated as love or compassion, "racham," appears 47 times in the Old Testament. It is translated as mercy or compassion 40 times but only once translated as love. Hence, the evidence strongly supports translating Psalm 18:1 as being compassionate to the Lord, which implies active involvement in His life. It may be difficult for believers to think about having compassion on the Lord, but Jesus taught believers how to show Him compassion (Matthew 25:34-40). When you minister to other believers by feeding the hungry, clothing the naked, inviting strangers into your home, or visiting those who are sick or in prison, you can do it unto the King: "One who is gracious to a poor man lends to the Lord, and He will repay him for his good deed" (Proverbs 19:17). Being compassionate to the King and His subjects will cause you to be blessed and inherit the kingdom.

Conclusions

Believers have authority through Jesus Christ to rule and reign in this life to influence the world in which they live (Romans 5:17). Just like Joseph, Esther and Daniel, believers must pray, fast and seek the Lord in order to operate with a kingdom spirit. The Father has called His children to a higher level in their daily walk with Him. In the days ahead, people will seek those believers who have a close relationship with the Lord for direction, comfort and wisdom. Only those believers with a kingdom spirit will be able to control the natural elements of this life through the power of God. Operating in a kingdom spirit will allow believers to have access and impact in the lives of others.

Chapter 5
BEST FOR THE FAMILY

The concept of "giving the best off the top for the family" was in the heart of God from the beginning. The names of the family members in God's family were written in the book of life before the world was created (Revelation 13:8). In order to reconcile God and man, the Lamb of God was slain in the heart of God before the world was created (Revelation 13:8). In other words, God gave the best He had – His only begotten Son (John 3:16) – from the beginning, or off the top, in order to have a family. Those people who have been the closest to God picked up this concept of giving. The concept goes by several names, such as the tenth, tithe, first fruits or seed, but it still refers to giving the best off the top for the family. Even though this is an important concept, many people do not regularly give the best off the top. The major deception keeping them from giving is fear. They fear that if they give off the top, there will not be enough to make it to the end of the pay period. This deception is addressed in this chapter by showing that the Lord can be trusted and that the benefits of giving the best off the top are too great to miss.

For purposes of this study, the term "tithe" will be considered as the most important approach used to practice the concept of giving the best off the top for the family. Tithing has been misunderstood and misused in the church world. The mighty biblical principle of tithing has been frequently condensed to a simple formula without any substance. Then God's people have been told that they would be debtors and robbers if they did not follow the formula. Therefore, people have felt obligated to follow the formula and fearful not to follow it. This formula is a miserable substitution for a relationship with the Lord Jesus Christ. The people who were fed lies about the glory of the formula are the ones who were robbed. They were robbed of their hope in Christ.

In reality, tithing is the spiritual instrument that can be used strategically to help fashion the future for you and your family. Tithing flows out of a heart filled with gratitude for what the Lord is doing and is expected to do in the future for you and your family. It is the seed being planted for a better future. It is the expression of your faith that appropriates the new covenant for you and your family. It touches heaven and opens a channel of blessings to impact your life and the lives of your loved ones.

Since tithing is an important way for believers to give the best off the top for their families, it will be the focus of this chapter. This chapter examines what it really means to give the best off the top. Tithing in the new season of prosperity will be analyzed with special emphasis on how it benefits the family and how it operates through the family.

Understanding the Tithe

This section examines the biblical foundation for the tithe. First, the initial tithes are shown to be closely related to family. Second, the expanded concept of the tithe as given in the Old Testament is examined. However, there are some aspects of the tithe as expressed in the Old Testament that are not relevant to Christians today. These issues are addressed as well. Third, the New Testament perspective on tithing is examined.

Tithing Introduced

The first recorded tithe was given by God's friend Abram (Genesis 14:20; James 2:23). He heard that a member of his own family, Lot, had been kidnapped (Genesis 14:1-16). He immediately assembled 318 trained fighters in his household and pursued Lot's captors, indicating that he was a man of strategic vision. God gave Abram a mighty victory over the enemy, which included the recovery of Lot and restoration of his possessions. As Abram returned from the battle, Melchizedek met him with food and drink. Apparently, Abram had sent word about the battle to Melchizedek, a spiritual person to whom he was connected. As priest of the Most High God, Melchizedek blessed Abram and blessed God (Genesis 14:18-20). Melchizedek made it clear that God had delivered Abram's enemies into his hands.

Recognizing that the great victory over his enemies and restoration of his family had been granted by God, Abram was moved to give a tenth, or tithe of all, to the priest Melchizedek (Genesis 14:20). Abram was thankful to God for restoring his family, and he was moved internally to tithe. No commandment had been given about tithing at that time. Abram tithed over 400 years before the law was given through Moses.

The tithe paid by Abram had immediate consequences. The Lord confirmed the covenant with Abram after the tithe (Genesis 14:20-15:21). At the beginning of Genesis 15 we learn the Lord would protect him and reward him greatly. The Lord confirmed that Abram would have a son of his own who would be his heir (verse 4). This tithe was a strategic move by Abram that had long-term implications for his family.

The second reference to a tithe in the scriptures was related to Jacob (Genesis 28:10-22). He used trickery and deceit to claim the birthright and blessing as his own (Genesis 26:27-34; 27:6-29). However, he had to flee from his family in fear for his life. Although most of the things had gone well for Jacob, his greatest concern was the separation from his family. He feared that he might never see his family again. The Lord appeared to Jacob in a dream and promised to give him and his family the land on which he was sleeping. Also, the Lord promised that his descendants would be too numerous to count. The encounter with the Lord, along with the promises related to his inheritance, his family and his descendants, moved Jacob to vow to tithe (Genesis 28:20-22). Jacob tithed approximately 300 years before the time of the law.

Abram tithed when his family was restored. Jacob tithed when the Lord promised to bless him and his family and to restore him to his father's house. Tithing is a biblical principle related to family from both a short-term and long-term perspective. Tithing did not begin or end with the law given to Moses.

Tithing Formalized and Expanded

The law which was given to Moses included commandments on tithing: "Thus all the tithe of the land, of the seed of the land or of the fruit of the tree, is the Lord's; it is holy to the

Lord" (Leviticus 27:30). The law continues, "For every tenth part of herd or flock, whatever passes under the rod, the tenth one shall be holy to the Lord" (Leviticus 27:32). The components of the tithe were identified as one tenth of the harvest or increase (Deuteronomy 14:22). Also, the tithe was described as being holy and belonging to the Lord. When the people were obedient to tithe, they could expect that things would go well for them and for their children (Deuteronomy 12:28).

Under the terms of the law, the Israelites were required to tithe to the Levites, whom God had chosen for the priesthood. The Levites had not been given an inheritance of land because the tithes were designated as their inheritance (Numbers 18:21). The tithes supported the Levites so that they could minister to the Lord and to His people. The Lord commanded that the Levites give a tenth of the tithes which they received – a tithe of the tithes – as an offering to the Lord (Numbers 18:26). The tithe was also to be used to care for the poor, including orphans, widows and foreigners (Deuteronomy 26:12).

The law imposed stiff penalties on people for failing to tithe, as we read in Deuteronomy 28:15: "But it shall come about, if you do not obey the Lord your God, to observe to do all His commandments and His statutes with which I charge you today, that all these curses will come upon you and overtake you." Furthermore, the book of Malachi explains that if a man does not tithe, he robs God and is cursed with a curse (Malachi 3:8-9). Therefore, people under the law were motivated to tithe out of obligation and in fear of the bad consequences of not tithing.

The New Testament differs radically from the Old Testament concerning tithing and these associated punishments. People who tithe according to the New Testament are to be led by the Holy Spirit in their giving rather than being under obligation to the law. Jesus Christ redeemed us from any curses associated with not tithing (Galatians 3:13-14). Tithing has to be understood from the perspective of the New Testament in order to be effective.

Tithing Refined

The New Testament has some direct references to tithing, and it also gives some much needed clarification. First of all, the New Testament does not do away with tithing. Instead, it explains that tithing is the right thing to do! Jesus taught that people ought to tithe (Matthew 23:23; Luke 11:42). Even legalistic tithes were affirmed by Jesus because that was all some people knew to do. However, there is a better way to tithe. It will be shown in this discussion that tithing motivated by love and given under the guidance of the Holy Spirit is very important.

The fear of punishment that the Old Testament law attached to tithing has been done away with in the New Testament. Tithing does not redeem us from the curse. Christ redeems us from the curse of the law (Galatians 3:13). However, legalistic giving has still been used in the church world to increase revenue and build institutions. Legalistic giving robs the believer of the responsibility to be guided by the Holy Spirit. Legalistic giving in the modern church takes away from caring for the needy in order to build institutions. This does not mean that tithing is contrary to the New Testament. Tithing is still very much a part of New Testament doctrine, but it must be done with the New Testament attitude and approach. Since the law and its ordinances and the priesthood have changed, the tithe has also changed.

The death of Jesus on the cross represents the ultimate tithe. He gave the best off the top for the family. He was sinless and innocent – the perfect sacrifice (2 Corinthians 5:21). He was cut down in the prime of life. His sacrifice demonstrated the greatest love (John 15:13). His death and resurrection reconciled God and man (2 Corinthians 5:19). His death and burial represented a seed being planted in the earth to produce a harvest. In this case, the harvest is the family of God. 1 Corinthians 15:20 states, "But now Christ has been raised from the dead, the first fruits of those who are asleep." He is the first fruits, and he has brought many sons into the family of God (Hebrews 2:10).

The tithe that Abraham (who was formerly known as Abram) gave to Melchizedek typifies new covenant giving to Christ (Hebrews 7:1-12). Tithing should be guided by the Holy Spirit; it should not be the result of following strict, legalistic formulas. Furthermore, tithing should come from a grateful heart (1 Thessalonians 5:18). Today, each believer should surrender all to Jesus Christ and give according to what the believer purposes in his/her heart: "Each one must do just as he has purposed in his heart, not grudgingly or under compulsion, for God loves a cheerful giver" (2 Corinthians 9:7). God does not want people to give grudgingly or out of necessity. The type of giving that God loves is cheerful, freewill giving. The New Testament clarifies that the true motive for tithing should be love. Giving which is motivated by anything other than love is unprofitable (1 Corinthians 13:3).

The most fascinating passage on tithing is given in Hebrews 7:1-12. Abraham gave a tithe to the priest Melchizedek, and Abraham is considered to be the father of all believers. He typifies those whose faith is in Jesus Christ. He sets the example for tithing by believers.

Earlier, it was shown that Abraham paid tithes in response to the victory that God had given him and the restoration of his family member, Lot. While restoration in his family may have motivated Abraham to pay tithes, the consequences of his tithe were far reaching. By tithing, Abraham symbolically paid tithes on behalf of his future descendants, the Levites. The Levitical priesthood would not be established until hundreds of years later, yet they symbolically paid their tithes through Abraham's tithe. This concept of linking a tithe in one time period to its impacts on future generations is an incredible one that can be applied by every Christian who understands and believes it.

Abraham had a long term strategic vision that included training and equipping his extended family. As we saw earlier, he trained 318 servants in his household to fight and each of these trained fighters were needed to rescue Lot. Abraham's tithe also had long-term consequences, producing future generations of men serving God. However, modern Christians tend to be short sighted and unwilling to sacrifice for long-term goals. If they understood the long-term consequences of tithing, their attitudes and actions would be radically different.

Applying the Tithe to Family

This section develops the concept of family and shows how natural families and spiritual families relate and interact. Tithing is the most important instrument that God uses to connect natural and spiritual families and to release eternal purposes in families.

Having healthy relationships in a natural family would help a person understand how to have a meaningful relationship with the invisible God. However, it is evident that the traditional, stable family is no longer dominant in modern society. The percentages of marriages ending in divorce and children being born out of wedlock are escalating at an alarming rate. This culture of dysfunctional families has produced the current fatherless generation.

Christ delivers us from the culture of dysfunctional families and joins us to a culture of family: "And if you belong to Christ, then you are Abraham's descendants, heirs according to the promise" (Galatians 3:29). He pours out the spirit of adoption to those who believe: "For you have not received a spirit of slavery leading to fear again, but you have received a spirit of adoption as sons by which we cry out, "Abba, Father!" (Romans 8:15).

In your spiritual family, you discover God as your Father and Jesus Christ as your brother: "Go to My brethren and say to them, 'I ascend to My Father and your Father, and My God and your God'" (John 20:17b). Through the spiritual family you learn the truth about the Father's love for you (John 14:23; 17:21-23). His unconditional love for you will never cease. He will never leave you nor forsake you (Hebrews 13:5). His love provides the acceptance and sense of belonging that all have longed for (Ephesians 1:6).

In your spiritual family, you discover God's people as fathers, mothers, sisters, brothers and children (Matthew 12:48-50; Mark 10:30). Fathers and mothers nurture and mature children.

Spiritual fathers help their children grow up (1 Corinthians 4:15). Spiritual mothers pray to birth Christ in their children (Galatians 4:19).

Considering the prevalence of abuse and perversion in natural families, it is not surprising that these things spill over into the church world. Some church leaders misuse the term "church family," while isolating the people and ruling by control and manipulation. The spirit of religion is manifested in controlling people, keeping them in bondage and not allowing Christ to be all that the people need. Church leaders controlled by the spirit of religion will try to build a wedge between the people and God so that the leaders and their institutions will seem to be valuable to the people. Otherwise, they cannot maintain their desired control over the people.

You can distinguish a true spiritual family from other so-called families by basic motivations. The motivation in a true spiritual family will be unconditional love. Christ will be all in all to the people with nothing else needed (Ephesians 1:23). In a spiritual family, the people are free and the Holy Spirit has liberty to move.

When the spiritual family functions as God intended, it will bring people together in love (2 Corinthians 5:18-20), nurture and mature them, and release them as ambassadors for Christ to God's purpose (Ephesians 4:11-16). Every member of the spiritual family, or every joint in the body of Christ, has something valuable to contribute to the environment of love and the process of maturity. Those people who have experienced a true spiritual family understand and appreciate the overall family of

God. They are ready and well equipped to reach out to all people to invite them to be a part of the family of God.

Believers want their natural families to be integrated into spiritual families by being born again and following the Lord. The greatest promise in the word of God is that your whole family can be saved: "They said, 'Believe in the Lord Jesus, and you will be saved, you and your household'" (Acts 16:31). The tithe can be used as the seed planted to integrate and promote natural and spiritual families. It can be used as a strategic instrument to bring forth the Father's desired purposes for you and your family.

Benefits from Tithing for Family

What can you do today to promote the future for you and your family? The tithe is the planting today that brings the harvest tomorrow. Your tithe can be used to fashion your future. If you live only for the moment then you will forfeit your influence over your future. The Lord plans to give you a hope and a future (Jeremiah 29:11). However, you have an important part to play in activating His plan for your future. You can do many natural things, such as invest and get an education, for the future. However, these natural things point toward a limited natural future. The tithe is a spiritual seed that brings forth an abundant spiritual future. Below is an example of a commitment to tithing that brought forth purpose and destiny in untold multitudes.

Our spiritual father, Brother Bob Terrell, had revelation knowledge about several important topics, including love, apostles and prophets and tithing. He developed and equipped numerous apostles and prophets who continue to walk in love and impact nations around the world. After Brother Bob started tithing, his wife showed him a budget with their income and expenses. Their expenses included housing, utilities, food, a car payment, etc. She showed him that they could not tithe and still pay their expenses from his income. Brother Bob analyzed the situation and drove 20 miles to the nearby town where he sold his Oldsmobile. He caught a ride home and announced that they would be able to tithe and still pay their expenses. Even though they lived 20 miles from town without a car, God met all their needs. Importantly, Brother Bob stayed true to his calling and his walk with the Lord. Because of his faithfulness, his ministry is reaching untold multitudes through the men and women he helped develop and equip for ministry. Brother Bob's influence in the kingdom is continuing more powerfully than ever before.

A practical example of the impact of tithing in our ministry is Jerold. He had many problems when we first met him, but the Lord delivered him using a process over time. Before coming to our ministry, he was admitted to mental facilities twelve times over a ten-year period. When he came to our ministry, he was addicted to drugs, alcohol and cigarettes and unable to keep a job. His family was on the streets without a home. The situation challenged people's thinking and their attitudes when they were confronted many times with the needs of Jerold and his family. The Lord provided food and shelter for him and his family in miraculous ways. He fell backwards several times, but we were there to show the Father's love and mercy. Over time, the Lord delivered him from addictions to drugs, alcohol and finally from cigarettes. He realized that his initial addiction to cigarettes opened a door to the forces of darkness. Throughout the process of his being delivered from addictions, he faithfully tithed, though he could only work for three months and then would go on a binge with drugs and be unemployed for eight months. This was a typical pattern repeated again and again. In our ministry, he learned more of the word of God and was delivered from many generational curses and addictions. Through this process he became a better worker and was able to keep a job. He is now a staff member at a drug rehabilitation center and a powerful minister, reaching out to people battling with addictions. His faithfulness to tithe resulted in financial freedom, as well as freedom from addictions.

What can you do to appropriate the new covenant? Through the new covenant, you are an heir of God and a joint heir of Christ (Romans 8:16-27). The Lord gives you the power to produce wealth in order to confirm His covenant (Deuteronomy 8:18). The tithe confirms the new covenant in your life. It confirms that the new covenant belongs to you and your family. Tithing is the instrument to activate your faith and appropriate the new covenant.

What can you do to touch heaven? The tithe releases the blessings from heaven to pour out on you and your family (Malachi 3:10-12). It releases your family from the enemy's grip and from all hindrances. It releases them so that your family can fulfill its destiny.

Tithing is an expression of thanksgiving for what the Heavenly Father is doing and will be doing in your life and in the lives of your family members. In other words, tithing is the corresponding action for a heart full of thanksgiving for family—what the family is and, more importantly, what it will become through Christ. When Abraham and Jacob started tithing, they both had much to be thankful for related to restoration in current family situations and relationships and to the blessings on future generations (Genesis 14:12-20; 28:13-22).

A thankful heart opens up a channel of blessings from heaven. For example, see how Jesus gave thanks to the Father before feeding the multitude (Matthew 15:36-38). Also, Jesus gave thanks at the last supper, recognizing the significance of His death on the cross and resurrection (Matthew 26:27). His death and resurrection gave birth to the family of God. Having a grateful heart helped Jesus fulfill His destiny. Likewise, your grateful heart, as expressed through tithing and the things that accompany it, will help you fulfill your destiny. It will also birth destiny in your family, both current and future family and both natural and spiritual family.

Exposing the Storehouse Deception

The greatest deception in the area of finances in the body of Christ relates to the concept of the storehouse. Ministers tell Christians to bring the tithe into the institution of the local church as the storehouse referred to in Malachi 3:10. However, the storehouse is not an institution, a structure, an organization or a program. The deception about the storehouse has its roots in a misunderstanding about the meaning of the word church. The word church actually refers to people, not an institution. The Greek word "ekklesia" which is translated as church throughout the New Testament means the called out ones. People build an institution and label it a church, but it is not a church according to biblical standards. Jesus is building His church, the called out ones (Matthew 16:18). The universal church (Ephesians 1:22) and the church in a city relate to people (1 Corinthians 1:2). When the people of Ephesus were called together to persecute Paul for casting out a demon, the word "ekklesia" was used to describe the gathering (Acts 19:32). This gathering of all people in the city was certainly not an institutional church but an assembly of people called out of the city. God's children are the church called out of the world, so they cannot "go to church." The church in a community gathers in a building, not a church, to worship the Lord.

The Hebrew word "owtsar," translated as storehouse in Malachi 3:10, means what is laid up, treasured or stored. Considering the treasure rather than the house gives a totally different perspective on what the Lord wants done with the tithe. The treasure is in earthen, meaning human, vessels (2 Corinthians 4:17). A storehouse relates to people being connected to one another through valuable relationships. While all believers are members of the family of God, many are not connected to other family members. Their names may be written on a membership roll for a local congregation without their having any real relationships with other believers. A storehouse cannot be a dysfunctional family in which people come to one or two services a week without being related to the other family members. The storehouse is a spiritual and functional family with treasure as measured by the anointed word of God and valued relationships.

Jesus had strong relationships with the 70 disciples and stronger relationships with the 12 apostles (Luke 10; Matthew 10). Jesus preached to the multitudes and taught them, but He did not pastor them. He did not have strong relationships with the multitudes. He described the multitudes as scattered sheep without pastors (Matthew 9:36). Today, ministers call themselves pastors of thousands, but they cannot have strong relationships with the multitudes. If Jesus could not pastor the multitudes, then certainly others cannot actually pastor multitudes.

The tithe is to be given where there are strong relationships, not just superficial ones. The tithe is put into the human vessel with the treasure of the anointed word of God and valued relationships. The person or people who pastor or father you are the vessels with the treasure. Those who pastor and father others must be able to touch their lives and call them by name at a minimum. It is not biblical for you to tithe to people who may stand in an office of pastor or apostle but have no real relationship with you. Do not tithe because of an obligation outside of relationships. Tithing outside of relationships has no value.

There are many problems associated with the deception of the storehouse being an institution, one of which is as follows. Ministers have perverted the concept of storehouse to store up grain (i.e., finances in this case) and build bigger barns. This perversion leads to hoarding the grain. When one storehouse gets full, they build bigger buildings. They do not build the church, which is people.

Explaining the Miracle of the Tithe

The tithe is much more than just bringing finances into the storehouse. Putting the tithe into the storehouse is spiritual, not carnal. The analogy of the water being turned to wine helps illustrate how the tithe works. Jesus' disciples filled the vessels with water, and the water was miraculously turned into wine (John 2:7-11). Then wine was given to the ruler for his approval.

As money, which is natural, is given along the lines of relationships to the human vessel as a tithe, it becomes spiritual. The woman with two copper coins gave her heart, soul and body to the Lord (Mark 12:41-44). By giving the two copper coins into the temple treasury, she gave the best, everything she owned. The two copper coins became greater than all of the offerings made by others. The others gave much out of their surplus. As the ruler of the temple, Jesus explained that the woman's little offering was turned into much. A miracle happened in her life! You can experience the same miracle of the tithe.

Tithing in the Family

To whom should the tithe be given? The tithe is for the spiritual family. Believers should tithe to the person, not the institution, who represents Christ and has spiritual authority in their lives. More specifically, tithe to the person who is responsible for helping you to mature and/or who is watching over your soul (Ephesians 4:11-13; Hebrews 13:17). If you want to prosper, then obey and support those that the Lord has set over you, so that their work can be fulfilled.

Those who preach the word of God are sowing spiritual seed that will produce a harvest in the lives of people. The one who sows the seed of the gospel has a right to share in the harvest (1 Corinthians 9:11). Those who preach the word of God should be supported by those who benefit from it (1 Corinthians 9:14). As a spiritual father, Paul asserted that he had a greater right to be supported by his own spiritual children than other preachers had (1 Corinthians 4:15; 1 Corinthians 9:11). Paul points out the importance of true relationships, such as a relationship between the father and his children.

Giving the tithe to pastors or spiritual fathers is not paying them wages. They are not hirelings working for wages. Their reward for sharing the word of life comes from heaven (John 4:32). You do not have to pay for oversight, nor can you be charged for oversight. Instead, you can believe and receive a harvest from the word of God growing mightily in your life. Therefore, you give the tithe out of a grateful heart to the one or ones who share the word of life with you.

Spending Finances from Tithes

How should tithes be used by those who receive them? The word of God does not give examples of tithes being used to build sanctuaries or buildings. Instead, freewill offerings were used to build sanctuaries and buildings (Exodus 36:3; 1 Chronicles 29:3-9). The finances associated with tithes are a blessing to those who receive them and should be spent as the Holy Spirit directs. These finances will help meet their financial needs and enable them financially to do the work of God. A pastor or spiritual father will use some of the finances provided by the tithes to care for the spiritual family. The concept of reaching out and helping people does not end with the family, but it certainly starts there. In the new season of prosperity, finances flow primarily along the lines of relationships within the spiritual family.

Conclusions

Many Christians tithe out of obligation to religious institutions. Such tithes help prop up the institutions. These people never realize the full benefits from tithing because they are not truly obeying God's commands. Following man's plan or the religious order in tithing is futile because it does not have God's blessings upon it. Tithing along the lines of strong spiritual relationships in accordance with God's plans releases enormous benefits which reach from generation to generation. You can help fashion the future and activate the new covenant for your family as you give the best off the top for the family.

Chapter 6

THE GOOD STEWARD

The person who is in charge of the household affairs for an estate is called a steward. The steward manages or oversees the property and finances belonging to another person. The concept of a steward applies to all believers, because they are given the responsibility to steward or manage the things of the Lord. All things were made by the Lord for His pleasure, including God's children (Revelation 4:11). You are not your own for you have been purchased with a great price – the life and blood of Jesus (1 Corinthians 6:19-20). The Lord owns your spirit, soul, and body, as well as all finances and the material things that you possess. Thus you have a responsibility to let people see Him in you.

The Lord calls His people to the high standard of being a good steward: "As each one has received a special gift, employ it in serving one another as good stewards of the manifold grace of God" (1 Peter 4:10). Do not be wasteful or slothful, but be a good steward of the riches which the Lord has given you. The Lord wants His children to be good stewards over His kingdom. A major deception in the area of stewardship relates to putting attention on worldly things rather than on the true riches of the eternal realm. The traditional Christian model of stewardship relates to how well a person handles finances and supports Christian institutions. A person does not need a lot of money in order to be a good steward from God's perspective. The objective of this chapter is to help you understand what it means to be a good steward. This study first describes the traits of a good steward. Then it examines how the good steward serves in the family of God and in the marketplace.

A Good Steward Described

The New Testament describes the good steward in much detail. The emphasis in the description of the good steward is on who he/she is and not what he/she does. A brief description of the good steward is presented in this section.

The good steward is faithful and trustworthy: "In this case, moreover, it is required of stewards that one be found trustworthy" (1 Corinthians 4:2). The good steward is wise, prudent and sensible: "And the Lord said, 'Who then is the faithful and sensible steward, whom his master will put in charge of His servants, to give them their rations at the proper time?'" (Luke 12:42). He/she must discern the evil from the good and follow those things that are of the Lord. He/she will have no part of those things that are evil. The passage Titus 1:7-9 gives several additional characteristics of the good steward. Briefly highlighting the passage, the good steward is not selfish, violent or greedy for money. The good steward is hospitable, a lover of good, sensible, just and self-controlled.

A person develops in character and grows in maturity to become a good steward. The word of God shows the process of growth and development that leads to godly character and spiritual maturity. Character is the set of inherent traits that define a person and guide his/her actions. Positive character traits include courage, dependability, respect, commitment, and integrity. The character trait of integrity guides the actions of doing what is right. In other words, a person of integrity would be expected to do what is right in every situation. Here are some important godly character traits: virtue (moral excellence), knowledge, self-control, steadfastness (patience, endurance), godliness, brotherly affection, and love (2 Peter 1:5-8). These godly character traits will make a person more productive and useful as a steward. Manifesting these godly character traits will make you a better representative of the Father in your dealings and relationships with other people.

A person can mature physically, emotionally, intellectually, and/or spiritually. While physical maturity relates to the passage of time, a believer may not mature spiritually even though several years pass. A person matures spiritually as he/she grows and develops in his/her relationship with the Lord. As a person matures spiritually, Christ becomes more evident in his/her life. Christ living in you gives you the assurance that you will share in His glory: "I have been crucified with Christ; and it is no longer I who live, but Christ lives in me; and the life which I now live in the flesh I live by faith in the Son of God, who loved me and gave Himself up for me" (Galatians 2:20).

Authority and Responsibility of Stewards

Jesus has all authority in heaven and earth (Matthew 28:18). He delegates authority to those whom He can trust, such as good stewards. Those stewards who are faithful and wise and do the Lord's will are put in charge of all His possessions (Luke 12:42-44). He can trust those who have proven themselves in the small things, finances, and the things of others. As people have shown themselves to be good stewards over the things that they have already received, they are prepared to receive more. A good steward will be recognized in any setting and promoted. A friend of Paul's was promoted to be a steward over the treasury of a city (Romans 16:23). As a good steward, you can expect to be recognized and rewarded for diligence and effectiveness.

Instructions for Spiritual Growth of Stewards

The word of God provides nourishment for your spirit man and renews your mind. Desire the sincere milk of the word of God so that you can grow (1 Peter 2:2). The Lord disciplines His sons by His Spirit and His word (Hebrews 12:5-7). Fivefold ministry gifts (apostles, prophets, evangelists, pastors and teachers) have been given to the body of Christ to mature and equip believers (Ephesians 4:11-16).

In one long discourse, Jesus discusses stewardship in much detail. He first tells his disciples about an unrighteous steward who had wasted his master's goods (Luke 16:1-8). This story introduced the problems that could arise from a person not being fit to be a steward. In particular, this steward was wasteful and dishonest. However, the unrighteous steward was commended for preparing for the future. Even worldly people with selfish motives prepare for the future, but God's own children have not been known for preparing for the future. The Lord has given much to His children that could be used to impact the future in a godly manner. It is a shameful commentary that Christians do not adequately prepare for the future.

Then Jesus provides great insights on preparing a person to be a good steward (Luke 16:8-16). There are three major character traits for good stewards that are evident in this passage: wisdom, faithfulness, and humility. As pointed out in verse 8, it is wise to build relationships, make friends and prepare for the future. In this passage, Jesus gives instructions on building relationships and making friends: use time, effort, and finances to invest in building relationships. Build relationships with people inside and outside the spiritual family. Relationship building will help strengthen and expand the universal and spiritual families. The Lord is interested first and foremost in people. Jesus was crucified and resurrected for family, so it is not surprising that He wants the attention of good stewards to be focused on people and families.

Jesus continues to instruct that a good steward must be faithful to God in little things, in finances, and in things that belong to other people. A person who is faithful in all the little things can be trusted with the things that really matter. A person who is faithful in finances can be trusted with true, spiritual riches. Natural possessions such as finances really belong to the Lord anyway. However, spiritual riches such as grace and the fruit of the Spirit belong to the believer. A good steward is faithful to God and values what is valuable to God.

As Jesus teaches in this passage about stewards, he encounters some people who were greedy for money. He knew the motives in their hearts (Luke 16:15-16). They wanted money to hoard up and spend on what they desired. This attitude of the heart is contrary to kingdom principles. A good steward must humble himself/herself and press into the kingdom: "Unless you are converted and become like children, you will not enter the kingdom of heaven" (Matthew 18:3b). A good steward functions in the kingdom and uses finances according to kingdom principles.

The Lord uses good stewards to birth and mature future generations of stewards so that they can receive their inheritances. Immature heirs of the kingdom are under guardians and stewards until the time determined by the Father (Galatians 4:1-2). As a good steward, Paul wanted every believer to mature in Christ (Colossians 1:25-29). The goal reflected a level of stewardship that is seldom seen in the body of Christ. It took the energy of God working through Paul to bring forth the Christ in other people. A major way of releasing this energy was through intercessory prayer. He travailed in intercession until Christ was formed in them (Galatians 4:19). A spiritual father, such as Paul, imparts character and maturity into believers.

Tests for Stewards

Stewards have grace to minister to others (1 Peter 4:10). They can minister through gracious words and gracious actions. God's grace, which is the operational power of the Holy Spirit, supernaturally empowers and energizes believers to live a victorious life. As long as believers function in the area where they have grace, they will be successful. However, believers cannot effectively minister grace to others until they have overcome some things in their own lives. Believers enter into stewardship by supernaturally overcoming. They must overcome natural circumstances in this life through supernatural means, as we read in Revelation 12:11: "And they overcame him because of the blood of the Lamb and because of the word of their testimony, and they did not love their life even when faced with death." Overcoming natural circumstances with natural abilities and resources is not the same thing as this biblical concept. Overcoming in a biblical sense involves the work of the cross, speaking the truth and centering on Jesus Christ. First, the blood of Jesus can be appropriated by believing the finished work of the cross upon which Jesus was crucified. His blood is precious and powerful enough to heal diseases and cast out demons. Second, the only effective testimonies involve speaking the truth as expressed in the word of God. Carnal people speak about things done in darkness because they do not have the word of God to bring light and life. As the anointed word of God is proclaimed by believers, it will change circumstances. Third, loving one's life involves selfishness. When a person loves his/her life that person's life becomes the center of everything. Focusing on Jesus Christ as the center of a person's life causes he/she to take on His desires. Then the person is motivated by His love, which is totally unselfish.

The caliber of each believer's stewardship is frequently being tested. Each challenge that a person faces can be considered a test. How well stewards meet the challenges determine whether they are good stewards. Good is the measure of a passing grade on a test, so stewards are rated as good whenever they pass their tests. The tests may relate to the daily affairs of life or difficult situations. The natural abilities of stewards are not adequate for the real tests. God's grace is needed to live an overcoming life. His grace is always sufficient (2 Corinthians 12:9). Even when you are weak, His grace is powerful. As long as you function where you have grace, you will be able to stand against any attack of the enemy and walk in victory.

The book of Job explains how one man overcame the catastrophes of losing his ten children and everything he owned. Job's life progressed from being a baby in the Lord to spiritual maturity. The Lord describes Job as blameless and upright from the beginning of the book (Job 1:8; 2:3). However, it is important to recall that the Lord speaks of those things that are not as though they were (Romans 4:17). The Lord sees the end of a thing from the beginning and calls forth the desired end. Job had integrity from the beginning of the story, but he lacked knowledge (Job 2:9-10). Knowledge is critical for overcoming any situation. Only at the end of the story did Job understand his true condition. The Lord confronted Job and rebuked him for speaking out of ignorance (Job 42:1-6). Then Job repented and thus changed his way of life.

Job matured spiritually by encountering the Lord, changing his life after being rebuked and overcoming the difficulties he experienced. Job overcame the tests that were put before him when he prayed for his so-called friends. They were called friends but they were more like his enemies. They spoke lies about him and to him. "The Lord restored the fortunes of Job when he prayed for his friends" (Job 42:10a). The Lord prospered Job and gave him twice as many riches as he had at the beginning. Applying the simple truths from Job's story to the lives of believers will help them overcome. His encounter with the Lord changed his life, and his reliance on spiritual things such as prayer caused him to prosper.

Overcoming Persistent Poverty

Why is the poor man poor? How do good stewards overcome challenges related to poverty? Major changes have to be made in lives in order to come out of poverty. Job's life and financial situation were changed after being rebuked by the Lord. Overcoming poverty relates to how well believers deal with conflicts, rebukes and instruction. Many people try to avoid conflict in all situations. This approach is like keeping your head down on a battlefield to avoid being shot. Keeping your head down in battle is not always an effective defensive strategy because you may not see what the enemy is doing. This strategy is also ineffective as an offensive strategy. It is better to face conflicts and resolve them than to ignore them. Without facing conflicts, many issues may remain unresolved so that a person is tormented inside. This approach does not allow them to bring issues to closure or to learn from conflicts. Open yourself up to the Lord and His people so that your course in life can be significantly changed. Let the Lord search your heart for everything that hinders your spiritual progress (Psalm 139:23-24). Develop the godly relationships that will help you prosper in every area of your life. Then give His ministers the right to speak into your life.

There are often important lessons to be learned from conflicts. A wise person will learn from conflict, even while being rebuked for mistakes (Proverbs 9:8; 13:1). Scoffers, arrogant people and the poor do not heed rebuke (Proverbs 13:1, 8). A poor man is poor because he will not heed instructions and make radical changes in his life that are needed to come out of poverty. In that respect, he is no different than an arrogant person or a scoffer. The truth that poor people do not heed rebuke is particularly relevant for understanding the long-lasting grip of poverty and the hindrances to prosperity. People who refuse to learn from rebukes and other conflicts remain poor. They often choose to keep doing the same things and remain poor rather than listen to correction. Correction is not pleasant when it happens, but later it yields fruit (Hebrews 12:11). However, correction yields fruit only if the person embraces it. Believers who want the true riches will listen to and heed correction and thereby produce much fruit. In other words, correction brings believers to a position in which they can prosper.

Overcoming Temporary Financial Problems

How do good stewards overcome challenges related to finances? A biblical principle showing how Jesus meets financial needs is evident in the miracles He used to feed the multitudes. When there was a need to feed the multitudes but little money to buy food, Jesus asked the disciples how many loaves of bread they had (Mark 6:38; 8:5). The disciples had only a few loaves. Jesus took and blessed these few loaves so that the disciples could feed thousands of men and their families (Mark 6:39-44; 8:6-9). Feeding thousands of people with just a few loaves of bread is a miracle. Jesus miraculously met these great needs using the disciples' limited resources. The pattern Jesus uses to meet financial needs is set and described with these miracles. Jesus takes and blesses a few things that believers have in order to meet their needs. Giving into the work of the kingdom of God is like sowing financial seed for a harvest. As you give under the guidance of the Holy Spirit, you can expect a harvest in financial blessings: "For whatever a man sows, that and that only is what he will reap" (Galatians 6:7b AMP). Job understood the principle of sowing and reaping because he helped the poor, the fatherless, the orphans, the lame and the blind (Job 29:12-16). He was blessed for these actions. Those who give generously will reap abundantly (2 Corinthians 9:6). God blesses what you give to Him and multiples it back to you.

Good stewards inquire of the Lord for guidance, operate in His grace by faith and obey His commands. How do you deal with challenges when your natural abilities are inadequate? If you rely on the blood of Jesus, the word on God and center your life on Jesus, you will be the good steward that Jesus wants you to be.

Stewardship Applications

Serving as a Good Steward in the Family

When people are born again, they become members of the universal family, or the household of God (Ephesians 3:15). The Lord then places each of them in a local family of God or spiritual family to develop relationships with other family members (1 Corinthians 12:18). Believers are to do good to all people, but especially to members of their own spiritual family. It is very important that you are good to your spiritual family (Galatians 6:10).

The good steward is first of all a steward of the riches within. He is a steward of God's grace: "Above all, keep fervent in your love for one another, because love covers a multitude of sins. Be hospitable to one another without complaint. As each one has received a special gift, employ it in serving one another as good stewards of the manifold grace of God" (1 Peter 4:8-10). In the original Greek text, these three verses include the same word that means one another, reciprocally, and mutual. Believers are to reciprocally and mutually love, and to share and serve one another in the spiritual family. As you have received grace, administer the same to your family.

Here is an example of the impact of good stewardship. Sherry and another minister, Cindy, were ministering in Honduras when the terrorists attacked the twin towers of the World Trade Center in New York City on September 11, 2001. She had flown on a Central American airline with plans to return home on September 13. However, none of the foreign airlines were allowed to fly into the United States for several days after the attacks. Sherry contacted the airline office each day to find out if she could return home. Each time she called, the people at the airline office said they did not know when their airplanes would be allowed to fly into the United States again. After several days of frustration, the Holy Spirit told me to receive my wife home. In a step of faith, I proclaimed that I was receiving my wife home. Then I contacted Sherry and told her what the Holy Spirit had instructed me to do. She knew that the time had arrived for her to fly home.

Sherry and Cindy packed their bags and went to the airport. Sherry said out of her mouth that God would provide the amount to pay the new ticket, which was over $600. There was only one plane from the airport flying into the United States on that day. They bought new tickets for the flight without knowing where it was going. Its destination was New Jersey near New York City. The plane circled over the site of the twin towers, and they saw the smoke rising from what remained of the towers. After landing, they were taken to a hotel where families were waiting for any news about survivors. As good stewards, Sherry and Cindy used the gifts within to pray for the families who lost loved ones in the terrorist attacks. When Sherry returned home, there was a check waiting for her that was the exact amount of the plane fare. A woman that we did not know very well had received some extra income and wanted to tithe on it to Sherry. She never tithed to us before or after this incident. However, her check for the amount of the airplane ticket showed the Father's faithfulness to meet the needs of His stewards who will go where He sends them.

Exhibiting the Kingdom in the Marketplace

Consider what the marketplace would be like if Christians walked in the Father's love, obeyed His word and followed His Spirit. People would really experience the Father's goodness and their lives would be changed forever. Broken hearts would be mended, the sick would be healed and the oppressed would be set free. Businesses, schools and government agencies would be far better places than they are now. You can be the catalyst for these changes in the marketplace where you work and shop. Be motivated by the Father's love in your dealings with others. Love never fails (1 Corinthians 13:8). Love will bring success to your relationships, career, business and investments.

Life with Jesus is an exciting adventure! Do not leave Him behind. Do not confine Him to your local congregation. Expect Jesus to be manifested through you everywhere you go. He is the word of God, wisdom and faith. As you speak the anointed word of God you will utter wisdom from above, activate your faith, and encourage the faith of others. You will live a long and successful life (Proverbs 3:1-2). You will be able to accumulate and disperse wealth according to kingdom priorities.

The Holy Spirit knows what lies ahead (John 16:13). He will guide you with respect to your education, career and investments. He will help you strengthen your family relationships, raise your children to serve the Lord, be creative on the job and invest wisely. The Holy Spirit can operate the spiritual gifts through you in any situation. The gifts of the Spirit are no longer to be limited to church services. The Holy Spirit wants to be manifested to the people you encounter on the job, in the supermarket, and everywhere else you go.

As a young professional, Sherry taught business education in a vocational school. After being married for twelve years, the Lord blessed us with three wonderful children in three and a half years. In order to have more control over her time to care for the children, Sherry resigned from the vocational school and started her own consulting business. She taught business and personnel management courses to managers and staff in private businesses and government agencies. She used godly wisdom and biblical principles to develop such programs as conflict resolution and personnel management and supervision, as well as stress management. She was able to minister to hurting people through her consulting business, often moving in the gifts of the Spirit to identify problems and solutions for individuals in her business seminars. Many people were healed, delivered and given godly advice in her business seminars. As the children grew older, she had more time to develop her consulting business and begin ministering to the homeless and oppressed. She ministers in church services, conferences, jails, prisons, etc. She travels widely in other countries, prophetically ministering God's word and bringing healing, deliverance and direction. It is not unusual for Sherry to pray for a sick person in a check-out line in a store and see the person healed. She often prophesies to people sitting at tables in a restaurant and sees the Lord move on them.

Conclusions

There are many vessels in the Lord's service. The pure golden vessels have gone through the fire, removing the impurities. Good stewards represent the pure golden vessels of honor that have no flaw and that stand up and declare that the Lord is God. These are the ones whom the Lord can use to do His bidding. They go where He sends and pour out life and hope to those with whom they come in contact. People are able to taste the Lord's goodness through these stewards. They leave goodness and mercy wherever they have been.

Chapter 7
EVER INCREASING ECONOMY

By faith Abraham looked for a city whose architect and builder was God (Hebrews 11:10). In Abraham's city the affairs of men would be positively impacted by heaven. Is Abraham's city a myth or a reality? People during his day and even today thought that he was a fool. However, Abraham's faith found the city for which he was seeking, for the word of God promises that a person finds what he seeks (Matthew 7:7). Abraham was looking for a city where heaven touched earth, making it a better place, and he found it. So who is the fool – the father of our faith – Abraham – or the skeptics? Abraham's city is the place where heaven touches people and the affairs of life, bringing abundance and increase.

Previous chapters have focused on the role of the individual in the family of God. This chapter focuses more on heaven's role in initiating and accomplishing God's purposes in the lives and affairs of family. The supernatural way of changing the lives and affairs of family is through a partnership between heaven and earth. This partnership is reflected in a supernatural economy of the family. Originally, the term economy meant management of the affairs of a household or family. The term economy has been extended to include the business affairs or economic system of an area or a nation.

A major deception related to the economy is that men think that they can develop a perfect economic system without God. This deception has been around at least since the tower of Babel (Genesis 11:1-9). Developing any economy apart from God is doomed for failure. In this chapter, the partnership between heaven and earth to impact the lives and affairs of family is called God's economy. His economy is continually increasing: "There will be no end to the increase of His government" (Isaiah 9:7a). When God touches the lives and affairs of family, He increases them and moves them forward for His eternal purposes.

The word of God has much to say about God's economy. However, the unified message on economy is generally overlooked because the Greek word for economy, "oikonomia," has been translated so many different ways in modern translations of the Bible. Recognizing that economy has been translated as stewardship, administration and dispensation will help you understand what the word of God says about it. The mystery of stewardship or economy of God's grace was revealed to Paul (Ephesians 3:2-3). Believers can understand this mystery by studying the letters which Paul wrote for the body of Christ (Ephesians 3:4). The unsearchable riches of Christ are contained in the mystery of God's economy (Ephesians 3:8-9). These passages explain that God's economy is a mystery which has been hidden in the past. However, God is now revealing the mystery through the word of God. The riches in God's economy are so great that they cannot be completely searched out nor can they be exhausted. These riches are available to all who understand this mystery.

Just as Abraham was on a quest for God's city and Paul was on a quest to understand the mystery of God's economy, we are on a quest for the manifestation of God's economy in our lives and families. This chapter will help you understand the supernatural realm where heaven touches earth. It will also help you understand how heaven can be called on to impact any situation concerning you and your family.

Supernatural Economy Described

There are two fully operational economies functioning today: the natural, worldly economy and the supernatural economy. As shown daily in the media, the world's economy is broken and cannot be fixed. On the other hand, the supernatural economy is growing stronger and stronger. Heaven touches earth in the supernatural economy. Bringing the supernatural from heaven into the natural realm alters the natural in order to accomplish God's eternal purposes.

The supernatural economy does not operate like the natural economy. It is important for believers to know how the supernatural economy operates, to be expecting heaven to touch their situations and to be sensitive to the supernatural realm. Without sensitivity, believers might never recognize that heaven touched their situations. A brief example will help show that there are great differences between thinking in heaven and thinking on earth. In a recent prayer meeting, we were asked to pray for a woman who had been taken to a hospital. We knew she was a Christian, but we did not know her physical condition. A prophetic word about the woman came forth during the prayer meeting: "All is well with her. She will be going home tomorrow." Based on this prophetic word, the natural mind would think that the medical staff would be able to help the woman so that she could return to her earthly home. Instead, she went to her heavenly home in accordance with the prophetic word. From heaven's perspective, everything was well with the woman because Jesus had prepared a heavenly place for her to live throughout eternity. The revelation of the word of God and the personal experiences presented in this chapter should help you understand the supernatural economy.

Its Nature

The supernatural economy relates to windows, doors and gates. The Heavenly Father has opened the windows of heaven and is pouring out blessings for you that will flow out to others. Go through the doors that the Father is opening unto you. You enter into the new structure of the supernatural economy through the door that can only be opened by the Holy Spirit, the porter (John 10:3).

The door is shutting upon one season and opening on another. It is like we are living in the days of Noah, when "they were eating, they were drinking, they were marrying, they were being given in marriage, until the day that Noah entered the ark, and the flood came and destroyed them all"(Luke 17:27). At this time a window in heaven, or portal, is opening. The rain of the Holy Spirit is coming upon the earth. A return to holiness shall be seen in God's children. This is the window of the Father's blessings. Just as in the days of Noah, some will be doing business as usual, not knowing that the flood of the Holy Spirit is at hand.

Be cautious, for every door is not of the Father. For the doors that He opens no man can shut, and the doors that He closes no man can open (Revelation 3:7). You will know without any doubt when the right door appears. You will have a confirmation by the Holy Spirit on which doors to go through. Doors that you have not expected will open, but you will know they are of the Father for there will be a witness of His Spirit (John 2:20, 27). Go through the doors that the Father has opened.

Watch for the door to a great and effective work which the Father is opening (1 Corinthians 16:9). Go forward as the Father commands. Do not depend on your own understanding or on your own strength. He looks on your heart and sees your desire to know His ways and His mysteries. As you go through the door, He will reveal His ways and His mysteries unto you.

Its Purpose

Doors will open in order to accomplish the Father's plan and purpose. The Father's plan shall prevail, and His will shall be accomplished. It is time to move into purpose and into the place that He has for you. It is a season of letting go of the things of the past and things that do not matter and move into the supernatural. All that is of man will be blown away. Store up treasure in heaven where the moth will not corrupt (Matthew 6:19-21). Put on your new clothing of righteousness (Revelation 19:8) and humility (1 Peter 5:5). The Father desires that His people come into His presence and see His wondrous glory. Motivations of the heart will be revealed, especially of those who would make merchandise of God's children. Exploitation of His children must cease.

The Father is supernatural, and He is manifested in the supernatural realm. However, people are looking for Him to move in other ways. In particular, people have a hunger to experience the spectacular. If they are only looking for Him to move in a spectacular way, they will miss their visitation. Focusing on carnal things distracts a person from being sensitive to the supernatural realm. The best way to experience the Father's visitation is to walk in the spiritual realm and to be stirred up every day by the Holy Spirit.

The Father speaks distinctly by His Spirit and by His anointed word to your heart or spirit man. First it's in your heart, and then it's in your hand. If you believe what the Father says to you, He will bring it to pass. A gift can be given, but it becomes a blessing only when it is received. Receive His word and trust that He will bring it to pass.

Keys to the Supernatural Economy

Prayer, praise and prophetic words can help a person tap into God's great power. Consider the case of Paul that is presented in Acts chapters 13 through 16. Paul was in a gathering of prophets and teachers who were fasting and worshiping the Lord. A prophetic word from the Holy Spirit was spoken by one of the prophets to separate Paul and Barnabas for the work of God (Acts 13:2-3). The prophets and teachers laid hands on them and sent them away. Then Paul and Barnabas traveled to several cities, proclaiming the word of God (Acts 14:3). The Lord confirmed the word they preached by granting them power for miraculous signs and wonders. Later the two men took separate paths, going to different cities and taking other ministers with them.

Paul then received specific instructions from the Lord in a vision to go to Macedonia (Acts 16:9). Soon after Paul and Silas arrived in Macedonia, Paul ministered in the area and cast a demon out of a slave girl, freeing her from bondage (Acts 16:18). However, this gracious act interfered with the plans of her masters to make money by using her as a fortune teller (Acts 16:19). Her masters persuaded the city officials to beat Paul and Silas and lock them in prison (Acts 16:20-24). Paul and Silas could have been downcast and complained about their situation. Instead, they chose to pray and praise the Lord (Acts 16:25). The Lord responded by granting a great outpouring of power to free them from prison: "And suddenly there came a great earthquake, so that the foundations of the prison house were shaken; and immediately all the doors were opened and everyone's chains were unfastened" (Acts 16:25).

From this passage, you might conclude that just prayer and praise were responsible for this outpouring of great power. However, both the prophetic word which separated Paul for the work of God and the vision which sent Paul and Silas specifically to Macedonia played an important part in releasing great power (Acts 16:9). Paul knew the importance of prophecies, visions and the doctrine of laying on of hands by anointed ministers. He instructed Timothy to stir up the gift which had been imparted to him by the laying on of hands because it would release the spirit of power (2 Timothy 1:6-7). In prison, Paul stirred up the gifts in himself which had been imparted by the prophets and teachers (Acts 13:3). When he prayed, praised the Lord and stirred up what had been imparted to him, the spirit of power was released to free him and the other prisoners. Such great power shook the foundation of the prison, opened every door and freed every prisoner (Acts 16:26). Paul was following the Holy Spirit by doing the Father's work in the place where he was instructed to go, so he had access to the Father's power. The prayers and praise activated the power. Likewise, if you are doing what the Lord called you to do in the place where He has sent you, then you have access to the power of God. Your prayers and praise will activate the power.

Prayer

Prayer can be used to initiate change in the lives and affairs of family. Through prayer you can ask for the changes which you desire. Prayer is the first line of communication between man and God. It is two-way communication: man speaking to God and God speaking to man. The Lord never sleeps but counsels and instructs believers day and night (Psalm 16:7). He is always ready to hear a believer's prayer: "The eyes of the LORD are toward the righteous and His ears are open to their cry" (Psalm 34:15). The Father does far above what is asked in prayer, according to the power of the Holy Spirit at work in the person asking (Ephesians 3:20). Such prayers will bring heaven's great power to bear on earth's problems (James 5:16).

According to the Old Testament, God's thoughts and ways are higher than those of man (Isaiah 55:8-9). However, the new covenant which is based on better promises gives believers access to the Father's thoughts and ways through His Spirit (1 Corinthians 2:8-10). The Father seeks a people who will put Him first, who will inquire of Him and will receive from Him. Watch and pray that you are not distracted by the thoughts and actions of men for the Father desires to share with you His thoughts, His plans and His desires. Set your affections on spiritual things (Colossians 3:1-2) and be not carnally minded, for that will bring destruction. Romans 8:6 states, "For the mind set on the flesh is death, but the mind set on the Spirit is life and peace." Watch and pray because it is time for signs and wonders to increase. Believe the Lord that you will be a part of that increase. Rid yourself of old thinking, for the Father does a new thing in the earth and in you (Isaiah 43:19; 2 Corinthians 5:17). You can pray and ask Him to increase your ability to listen to His Spirit. Then you can be led by the Holy Spirit and operate with the mind of Christ (1 Corinthians 2:16; Philippians 2:5).

There are two types of prayer: the prayer of doubt and unbelief and the prayer of faith. The prayer of doubt and unbelief is based on traditions of men and the doctrines of men and devils. Such traditions and doctrines make the word of God ineffective in the lives of those who rely on such things (Mark 7:13). Prayers outside the word of God and without the guidance of the Holy Spirit are ineffective. The prayer of doubt and unbelief is a waste of time. On the other hand, the prayer of faith is effective (James 5:15). Whatever you ask in the name of Jesus will be done by the Father (John 16:23). The prayer of faith never fails!

Praise

For believers, praise is a heart-felt expression of love, adoration and thanksgiving to God. The Lord Jesus Christ is worthy of all praise. Through His death He paid the ultimate sacrifice to redeem us, and through His resurrection He gave us new life. Praise magnifies the Lord and makes Him big in your life (Psalm 34:3). The highest form of praise is imitation, so your highest praise to the Lord would be to reflect godly character traits such as love, humility and faith. As you develop in character and grow in maturity in order for Christ to be manifested in your life, you really express praise to the Lord. Just singing praise songs or listening to others sing praise songs is not real praise if your heart is not right. Jesus clarifies this in Matthew 15:8, "This people honors Me with their lips, but their hearts are far away from Me." Praise acknowledges that Jesus has preeminence in your life (Colossians 1:18). Through praise you humble yourself under His mighty hand (1 Peter 5:6).

The Lord inhabits the praises of His people: "Yet You are holy, O You who are enthroned upon the praises of Israel" (Psalm 22:3). Even though this scripture refers to God's chosen people, Israel, it applies to all Christians because we have been grafted into Israel (Romans 11:11-19). Therefore, the Lord will inhabit the praises of believers. Rather than coming to dwell on the earth, the Lord raises up His people through the Spirit to fellowship in His presence. Through praise, you can have intimate fellowship with the Lord. His presence is to be a haven of peace and rest.

You can offer the sacrifice of praise and make the Lord bigger than your natural situation. In difficult times you can choose to praise sacrificially even when you do not feel like it. Sacrificial praise shows that you believe in Him and want to please Him (Hebrews 13:15). Do not let praises unto the Lord cease from coming out of your mouth for He has ordained praise as your strength (Psalm 8:2; Matthew 21:16). Do not allow distractions or hindrances to keep you from praising the Lord. Praise to the Lord brings the anointing and the refreshing of the Lord's presence.

Praise should be a way of life. Cease not to praise the Lord. "I will bless the Lord at all times; His praise shall continually be in my mouth," says the psalmist (Psalm 34:1). If you can turn praise on in the presence of other people and then turn it off later, you are not praising Him continually.

There are two types of praise: false praise and true praise. False praise covers over the unrighteous motives of the heart. Some people want to please man rather than God. Their praises are an outward show (Matthew 15:8). Jesus knows whether people praise Him with their heart. True praise reveals the motives of the heart as sincere devotion and humility. True praise brings you into the presence and power of God (Psalm 100:4). Praise raises you up into the supernatural realm of life and into the power of God. Lifting up Jesus Christ through praise activates His power to flow in you, through you, and around you. Paul and Silas knew how to lift their hearts above their circumstances and enter into God's presence and power (Acts 16:25-26). Their praise opened a portal for His power to alter their situation by freeing them from prison. Through praise you can have intimate fellowship with the Lord and experience His great power.

Prophetic Word

One of the major instruments that the Lord uses to initiate change in the natural realm is the prophetic word. The prophetic word releases potential on earth to fulfill the Father's purposes. The prophetic sees the invisible and brings those things into this time dimension. The prophetic voice calls those things that are not as though they were (Romans 4:17). For example, the prophet Abraham (Genesis 20:7) saw Jesus' day and rejoiced in it (John 8:56). He saw Jesus among his descendants. By believing and obeying the word of the Lord, Abraham made it possible for Christ to come forth in his family. You are to look beyond the circumstances in your life and family and see Jesus as victorious over your situation (Hebrews 12:2).

The Lord is building a supernatural economy on the earth. The prophetic voice, which represents the Father's will, lays out the pattern for the building. Until the Father's will for something is prophesied, it cannot be built. Once it is prophesied then the Lord will bring it to pass (Jeremiah 1:12). The prophetic voice gives direction. The prophetic voice brings life, increase and comfort. Bringing comfort and hope helps establish the hearts of people. The prophetic voice is becoming stronger.

The prophetic voice first utters and then the gate opens wide. For example, a severe famine occurred in Samaria because the city was under siege (2 Kings 6:25-7:20). Elisha had been teaching, just doing things as usual. However, the people needed a breakthrough. The letter of the law kills, but the Spirit brings forth life (2 Corinthians 3:6). A true prophet only speaks the Father's word as the Spirit wills. Elisha prophesied that food would be abundant and prices would be low the next day (2 Kings 7:1). Elisha released a prophetic word which caused a shift in heaven to occur. The city gate was opened wide, and the people rushed out to spoil the enemy's tents and bring back an abundance of food to the city. Food prices were low the next day just as Elisha had prophesied (2 Kings 7:18).

A prophet carries a great responsibility, because a prophet speaks for the Lord. The Lord's words are like a pure stream of water. The Lord will not allow His word to be polluted. Polluted word means that it has been mixed with carnal thinking. Carnality pollutes! Jesus taught that you should consider carefully what you hear (Mark 4:24) and how you hear it (Luke 8:18). You are to hear with your spirit man, because the spirit man can discern the Father's word. The anointing of the Holy Spirit will teach and protect the believer (1 John 2:20, 27).

The King's commands must be obeyed. With a command you have no choice. However, with a prophetic call to action you have a choice to obey or not to obey. Obedience to a prophetic call to action brings blessings from heaven.

Operating in the Supernatural Economy

Believers can prosper through the Father's supernatural economy. They are in the world but not of the world (John 17:11, 16). Believers are citizens of heaven and have rights and privileges associated with their citizenship in heaven. Believers have been recreated to walk in the spiritual realm. The Father is calling His children to move to a higher realm in Him. As they follow His Spirit, they will prosper. As they follow His Spirit, they can have their needs and wants met (Philippians 4:19; 2 Corinthians 9:8). The Lord Jesus has set you free, so do not return to the old order that was made of rules and regulations that hinder the movement of His Spirit. Move with His Spirit step by step and day by day. The Father desires to lead you to a higher level on His holy mountain. Trust not in man and flattering lips but trust in the

Father and you will do exploits in His name. He is getting you ready to see the mighty, wonderful things that He will do for those who believe.

Begin to move in the realm of power! Do not waver. A person who doubts or wavers does not receive the Father's favor (James 1:6-8). Stand fast in agreement with His plan and purpose. You must believe in order to see the working of miracles. Faith sees what the Father is doing and what He wants to establish in the natural realm.

If you walk with the Father, He will provide shelter for you and cause you to walk in a higher realm with more power. Seek those things which are from above and which glorify the Lord (Colossians 3:1-2). The heavenly realm is open and accessible to believers through Jesus Christ (Hebrews 4:14-16). Believers are encouraged to experience the heavenly realm by coming to the Father's throne to receive mercy and grace. Walking in the Father's mercy and grace is evidence that you have experienced the heavenly realm. Below are two examples that show that the supernatural economy belongs to those who seek it.

When our daughter, Amy, made plans to marry, we asked the Lord for the money to pay for her wedding. Then a staff member from the National Academies of Science, Engineering and Medicine called and asked me to finish a research report for them. Scientists from all over the nation had worked on the project for several months. The staff at the National Academies did not have the expertise to complete the report on their own. They asked me to fly into the Washington, D.C. area to work on the report. I was picked up at the airport by a driver with a limousine and carried to meet with those staff members who were working on the report. I edited the report by reorganizing it, adding material to it and omitting some of the existing material. Then I flew back home. When the work was finished, I received a check for thousands of dollars and presented it to Amy for the wedding. Without a doubt, this money was provided by the Lord for Amy's wedding. Incidentally, she had a beautiful wedding that we will always remember. We are thankful for the Father answering our prayers!

In another instance, I published a research article on the growth and stability of government finances in the National Tax Journal. A government employee from Prince Edward Island in Canada read the article and asked me to analyze the financial situation for his government. He sent me some data which I analyzed. I sent him the results that he requested. It was an easy task to complete. After the work was done, he mailed me a check for $2100. Before the check arrived, the Holy Spirit said this was the sevenfold return that we had been expecting. Earlier, we had to pay $300 for car repairs. We knew that the enemy had stolen the $300 from us, so we claimed a sevenfold return as promised by the Lord in Proverbs 6:30-31. We never would have connected the two events, but the Holy Spirit connected them. Evidently, the Holy Spirit had moved on the heart of a person in Canada to send me the sevenfold return on the money that the enemy had stolen from us. The Lord is faithful and His promises are sure!

Conclusions

Heaven has whatever you need. If you need security, peace of mind or financial freedom, look unto Jesus. The Father will meet all your needs through Jesus. The windows of heaven are open and the blessings are being poured out as a mighty river through the Father's ever increasing economy. Every place heaven touches earth, the flow of blessings brings increase and abundance. Hoarding blocks the flow of the ever increasing economy. The flow can be initiated with prayer and prophetic words. The flow can be activated, increased and sustained through prayer and praise. Real and lasting changes in lives and situations are produced wherever this flow from heaven touches earth.

Chapter 8
A LASTING LEGACY FOR FAMILY

A legacy is something left behind. It is something significant handed down to a successor. A legacy connects one generation to succeeding generations. You can leave a legacy to your children and grandchildren. You can leave a legacy to your spiritual children. Your legacy can impact generations.

A legacy could include an inheritance, a birth right, a blessing, and the birth of character. While a natural inheritance can be very important, natural inheritances will not be considered here. This chapter will deal only with significant, spiritual legacies. Leaving a lasting legacy benefits both the person leaving the legacy and the people receiving it as their inheritance. The legacy can become the finishing touch or the ultimate achievement for fulfilling destiny for the person leaving it. It can help those who receive it live a more abundant life. It also can become a building block for fulfilling destiny for those who receive it. A major deception in the area of legacy relates to emphasizing natural legacies and thus considering spiritual legacies less important than they really are. This chapter examines the importance of spiritual legacies and shows how you can leave a lasting legacy to your natural and/or spiritual family.

A person in one generation can receive an inheritance from a previous generation and then pass what was received along to the next generation. The kingdom of God endures from generation to generation (Daniel 4:34). God's people are stewards of His kingdom and are expected to pass it along from one generation to the next. Even though a person does not have a natural family from which to receive an inheritance, he/she can receive one by being in the family of God (Galatians 3:13-14). What a person received as an inheritance in the family of God can be passed along as a legacy to the next generation of his natural and/or spiritual family.

Brother Bob Terrell, our spiritual father, birthed purpose and destiny in our lives. It was his legacy for us. As a result of being connected with Brother Bob and the men around him, we were able to start on a path to fulfill our own purpose and destiny. Many people contributed to our spiritual walk. Without them we would have missed the reason for our being on the earth. Having received Brother Bob's legacy as our inheritance, we want others to know the importance of a legacy.

Receiving an inheritance from previous generations is not restricted to the people you know. For example, Smith Wigglesworth (1859-1947) was a powerful minister who lived in England in the early twentieth century. He raised at least 14 people from the dead. He had such a strong anointing that when sinners came into his presence they would begin to cry out for the Lord to save them. He was described as an apostle of faith. We read many books about Smith Wigglesworth and the messages he preached. His life and revelation impacted our lives in the areas of faith and healing. Once we were in a meeting and a minister was introduced as having been close to Smith Wigglesworth. Her parents had been married by him, and she had been close to him as she grew from a child to an adult. He had prayed for her and laid hands on her to impart some spiritual gifts. After the woman was introduced, Sherry began running from the back of a large auditorium with hundreds of people. Sherry ran up to the minister and embraced her, because she wanted everything that the woman had received from Smith Wigglesworth. It became part of Sherry's inheritance. The sons turning their hearts to the fathers in previous generations and the fathers turning their hearts to the sons fulfill legacies.

The Pattern for Leaving Legacy

Many people in the word of God left a legacy to subsequent generations. Abel still speaks to us by his example of faith and righteousness (Hebrews 11:4). His legacy is eternal. A few interesting examples relating to a legacy will be considered in this section. These examples show a clear pattern for leaving a lasting legacy.

Legacies of the Patriarchs

The patriarchs – Abraham, Isaac and Jacob – left important legacies. Each of their legacies was given by faith and received by faith by their families. Abraham's legacy brought an innumerable company of sons into the family of God. "In your seed all the nations of the earth shall be blessed, because you have obeyed My voice," says Genesis 22:18. Abraham saw Jesus Christ as his descendant and rejoiced greatly (John 8:56). If you belong to

Christ then you are Abraham's descendent and heir to God's promises (Galatians 3:29).

Isaac and Jacob acted in faith to impart legacies by blessing their children and grandchildren, as Hebrews 11:20 tells us: "By faith Isaac blessed Jacob and Esau, even regarding things to come." Isaac was deceived as he blessed his youngest son Jacob. When his firstborn Esau asked for the blessing, he found out that it could not be taken back (Genesis 27:33). Once a legacy has been given, it cannot be stolen. "By faith Jacob, as he was dying, blessed each of the sons of Joseph, and worshiped, leaning on the top of his staff" (Hebrews 11:21). Jacob gave the birthright of a double portion to Joseph rather than to his firstborn son Reuben. He had the right to choose who would receive his legacy.

Some Other Old Testament Examples of Legacy

A person leaves a legacy to those with whom he has a close relationship and those who desire the legacy. Elijah trained and equipped Elisha, and Elisha faithfully served him (1 Kings 19:19-21). When the time approached for Elijah to be caught up to heaven, Elijah asked what Elisha wanted from him. Elisha named the legacy that Elijah would give him. He called forth the double portion: "Please, let a double portion of your spirit be upon me" (2 Kings 2:9). Elijah set a requirement for Elisha to meet in order to receive the legacy: "If you see me when I am taken from you, it shall be so for you; but if not, it shall not be so" (2 Kings 2:10b). Elisha had to stay close to Elijah until the end. Likewise, a person has to stay close to the one who will leave a legacy in order to receive it.

King David desired to build a temple for God's dwelling place on the earth. When he was unable to build the temple himself, he left a remarkable legacy to his son Solomon for him to build the temple. David gave Solomon the plan of God for the temple and its rooms, the buildings around the temple and the precious utensils (1 Chronicles 28:11-18). David and his leaders provided gold and silver for the utensils of the temple. David gave Solomon directions on how to involve others in building the temple and providing service in the temple. Like David you can help people in the next generation advance the kingdom of God.

Jesus Instructed About Legacy

The person with a legacy offers it to those whom he chooses. People who are not chosen to receive an inheritance from their family often try to overturn the decision on distributing the inheritance. One man asked Jesus to change the distribution of his family inheritance so that he could receive some of it (Luke 12:13-15). Jesus would not overturn the decision about who would receive the family inheritance. He will not take away the right of the family to choose who receives their legacy. You cannot obtain someone's spiritual legacy without their approval.

In the story of the prodigal son, the father provided a legacy for both of his sons (Luke 15:11-32). Everything that the father owned belonged to his two sons (verse 31). The younger son took the natural inheritance and wasted it, but later he returned to his father and received the real inheritance (verses 12-24). While the father's legacy was offered to both sons (verse 12), the older son did not take advantage of it (verse 29). Even though the older son stayed with the father and worked in his fields, he did not receive the father's legacy that was offered to him.

Jesus' Legacy at The Last Supper

Preaching and teaching the word of God plants seeds in the lives of people. Then the Lord watches over His word to bring forth fruit (1 Corinthians 3:6). However, preaching and teaching are not the legacy being considered here. Jesus taught the multitudes, but He left a legacy to the twelve apostles that He did not leave to the rest of His disciples (Matthew 26:20-29). At His last supper, Jesus entrusted the legacy of His body and blood to the twelve:

> While they were eating, Jesus took some bread, and after a blessing, He broke it and gave it to the disciples, and said, "Take, eat; this is My body."
>
> And when He had taken a cup and given thanks, He gave it to them, saying, "Drink from it, all of you; for this is My blood of the covenant, which is poured out for many for forgiveness of sins." (Matthew 26:26-28)

The legacy of His body and blood was extended to those twelve with whom Jesus had a close relationship. Eleven received the legacy, but one rejected it (Luke 22:19-21). Judas had been with Jesus throughout His ministry, but at the end he rejected Jesus and everything that Jesus offered him. It is a terrible thing to reject a legacy that is being freely offered. The apostles who received the legacy of the blood and body of Jesus freely passed it on to countless others in all future generations.

Faith, Hope And Love Remain

There are three things that remain – faith, hope and love (1 Corinthians 13:13). This is the season to come into increased faith, increased hope and increased love, for the Lord is faith, hope and love. He remains as faith, hope and love, for He does not change. These three are components of the fruit of the Spirit. Likewise, the other components of the fruit of the Spirit remain (John 15:16). Jesus chose you to bring forth fruit that would remain.

Legacy of Faith

Faith can be passed from one generation to another as a legacy of faith. Timothy's grandmother Lois and his mother Eunice deposited faith in him: "For I am mindful of the sincere faith within you, which first dwelt in your grandmother Lois and your mother Eunice, and I am sure that it is in you as well" (2 Timothy 1:5). The deposit of faith was their legacy to Timothy. A legacy can include faith that is passed from generation to generation.

To be effective, a legacy of faith must be given to those who are qualified to receive it. "When there is a man who has labored with wisdom, knowledge and skill, then he gives his legacy to one who has not labored with them. This too is vanity and a great evil" (Ecclesiastes 2:21). Trying to deposit a legacy of faith in people who are not qualified for the gift would be wasteful and unproductive. Moreover, wasting a legacy of faith is a great evil.

When Paul chose Timothy to disciple and equip, he already had a good reputation among believers in the region in which he lived (Acts 16:1-2). Deposit faith in those who are qualified to receive it and to pass it along to others: "The things which you have heard from me in the presence of many witnesses, entrust these to faithful men who will be able to teach others also" (2 Timothy 2:2). Faith is the direct result of receiving instruction from the word of God (Romans 10:17).

Legacy of Hope

The new season is a time of hope. Hope is a confident expectation that the promises in God's word belong to us. Romans 15:13 tells us, "Now may the God of hope fill you with all joy and peace in believing, so that you will abound in hope by the power of the Holy Spirit." This hope is a steadfast anchor of the soul that touches the presence of the Lord (Hebrews 6:19). The anchor holds on to the reality of God's promises. The basis of your hope lies in God, not in yourself. Trusting the Lord can give you the anchor upon which you can rely.

The Lord promised Abram that he would become the father of many nations (Genesis 15:5). However, Abram followed the carnal nature and had a child from a slave woman (Genesis 16), but this son was not through the promise. To confirm the promise, the Lord changed Abram's name to Abraham, which means father of a multitude (Genesis 17:5). When Abraham was almost an hundred years old, he had no human reason to hope in having a child to fulfill the Lord's promise (Romans 4:17-21). However, he continued to hold on to the promise and hope in faith that he would become the father of many nations. The Lord was faithful, for Abraham and his wife Sarah had a son, Isaac, through the promise. Like Abraham, you can hold on to everything that the Lord promises you through your spirit man or a prophetic word. The prophetic word brings comfort and hope and establishes the heart to receive the Lord's promises.

The highest hope is to stand in the place of grace and glory (Romans 5:1-5). Jesus Christ gives believers access to this place through faith (verse 2). Grace is the active power or energy of the Holy Spirit operating through a believer. Glory is the manifest presence of the Lord and His abundance. In this place you have victory over all trials, troubles and problems (verse 3). In this place you experience the Father's provision and protection. Then, you can draw on these victories that you experienced over your lifetime and you can hope for victory in every situation that you face (verse 4). You can hope for the Father's provisions to meet your needs. Even in the darkest hour, you can have hope where others have no hope. This hope never results in disappointment (verse 5). You can witness to others about the blessings that you have experienced in Jesus. Witnessing about these experiences will stir up hope in others.

Always be ready to answer anyone who asks about the hope that is within you (1 Peter 3:15). Passing your hope along to others will allow your hope to continue: "Know that wisdom is thus [sweet as honey] for your soul; if you find it, then there will be a future, and your hope will not be cut off" (Proverbs 24:14). As Paul wrote, subsequent generations can become your hope and joy (1 Thessalonians 2:19). You can leave a legacy of hope by sharing hope with others.

Legacy of Love

Paul blessed his son Timothy and explained that the goal of his teaching was for Timothy to grow in love: "But the goal of our instruction is love from a pure heart and a good conscience and a sincere faith" (1 Timothy 1:5). As Paul left a legacy of love for Timothy, you can leave a legacy of love to others.

From an early age, I had a love for the people of God, especially those who looked like me and talked like me. When we started ministering to children in low-income areas, I realized that my love was limited. In order to follow Jesus, I had to walk in greater love. The Lord deposited love in my heart at the mission where we fed and ministered to the homeless. I am supernaturally able to love all people, including the unlovely, the poor and the outcasts. Now I compassionately minister to people in jails, prisons and developing countries.

Early in our ministry, Jesus told us that only one thing was required – love. We had to love the people unconditionally as Jesus loved us. Through the love that the Holy Spirit deposited in our hearts, we are leaving a legacy of love to those around us.

Imparting Legacy

This is the season to bring faith, hope and love to the world. The purpose of imparting legacy is to bring forth the faith, hope and love of the future generation. Believers should readily impart those things received from God to others – "For I long to see you so that I may impart some spiritual gift to you, that you may be established" (Romans 1:11). If you have been redeemed by the blood of Jesus then you should treat people the same way you want them to treat you (Matthew 7:12).

Paul's goal of bringing everyone to perfection in Christ Jesus (Colossians 1:28) is one of the most remarkable statements in the

Bible. At any point in time every group of believers will include some mature and some immature believers. However, these groups could represent different generations. People can mature in their generation according to God's plan and purpose. Even though Paul's goal seems like an insurmountable task, he showed how it was to be accomplished in the next verse: "For this purpose also I labor, striving according to His power, which mightily works within me" (Colossians 1:29). The power of God was energized and at work in Paul to accomplish the task. It was Christ in Paul bringing forth Christ in others in their generation. Likewise, Christ in you can bring forth Christ in others in their generation. When you realize that it is Christ working in you, then you are not under pressure to perform. The apparently insurmountable task of maturing others becomes possible through Christ.

There are several ways to impart a spiritual legacy. The spiritual legacy comes from the heart through the mouth. Let everything that you say and do be done from the heart as unto the Lord Jesus (Colossians 3:23). Let the Holy Spirit guide and empower you in everything you say and do (Romans 8:14; Acts 1:8).

A Lifestyle of Imparting Legacy

The first way to impart legacy is through touching life together. Be useful and profitable to other people (Galatians 6:10 AMP). Deliberately add value to their lives by listening, caring and encouraging. This approach includes spending quality time together in fellowship, discussing the word of God and sharing issues of the heart: "They were continually devoting themselves to the apostles' teaching and to fellowship, to the breaking of bread and to prayer" (Acts 2:42). Then the Lord added to their fellowship. As you fellowship with others, you can comfort and encourage them with the comfort and encouragement that you received from the Lord (2 Corinthians 1:4). Touching life together is an important way to impart legacy.

Special Ministry to Impart Legacy

Declaring a spiritual blessing over successors can release destiny and purpose in their lives. Jacob called his twelve sons together and spoke a blessing over each of them (Genesis 49:1-33). The blessings were unique and appropriate for them and their descendants. For example, the blessing of Judah brought forth the ruler from his branch of the family (verse 10). This prophecy pointed to Jesus who is the Lion that belongs to the tribe of Judah (Revelation 5:5).

Legacies may relate to spiritual gifts. Some spiritual gifts exist in the lives of people from the time they are born. For example, some people may have a prophetic gifting before they are born again. Their keen insight into the future may be used either for good or evil. When people are born again, they receive spiritual gifts by Jesus and the Holy Spirit coming into their lives. These gifts can lie dormant until they are activated and developed. Believers can help stir up and develop spiritual gifts in other believers as a part of their legacy for others. Furthermore, ministers can pray, prophesy and lay hands on people to impart spiritual legacy (Acts 13:1-3). While the gifts are from the Holy Spirit, the roles of ministers are critical: "Do not neglect the gift which is in you, [that special inward endowment] which was directly imparted to you [by the Holy Spirit] by prophetic utterance when the elders laid their hands upon you [at your ordination]" (1 Timothy 4:14 AMP).

Conclusions

This is the season for the hearts of the fathers to be turned to the children and the hearts of the children to be turned to the fathers (Malachi 4:6; Luke 1:17). Wisdom connects generations. It is wise to embrace the truth of past generations, to walk in the present truth, and then to leave a rich legacy to future generations.

In order to have a spiritual legacy it is important to receive someone's legacy as your inheritance. Some people who are further along in their spiritual walk have something to contribute to you. Pray for divine connections with earlier generations. Ask the Holy Spirit to identify the people from whom you are to receive their legacy as your inheritance. Pursue a relationship with them. Be a true friend and a valuable contributor to the relationship. Let it be known that you want to receive their legacy as your inheritance. Touch life with those in the previous generation!

Walk in the spirit producing fruit that will remain and that will be recognized by others as being valuable. Your legacy for others will be generated from your fruit that remains. Identify the legacy that you want to leave to someone. Developing the legacy can be a lifelong endeavor that goes along with your maturing in Christ and your developing in godly character. Pray for divine connections with young people. Ask the Holy Spirit to identify the people to whom you are to leave a legacy. Reach out to those people by developing strong relationships with them. Let them know that you want to leave your legacy to them. Touch life with those in future generations!

Chapter 9

THE NEW FEAST: INTIMACY

When Jesus comes into a person's life, He makes that person rich. Then the person needs to learn what it means to be rich in the Lord. The rest of his/her life can be spent searching out the full riches, which are eternal, in order to walk in them. However, many people miss the eternal riches and spend their lives searching for temporal riches. Some people sit in congregations where they are not receiving the full riches because the true meat and drink offerings have been cut off. Many appear to be satisfied with the crumbs rather than with the abundance which is available in Jesus (Luke 16:21). However, the Lord wants believers to experience abundance in every area of their lives.

Come and dine at the Lord's Table. All things have been prepared for the feast. Every time believers come into the presence of the Lord and begin to feast with Him, they are immersed in His glory and filled with His joy (1 Peter 1:8; Jude 1:24). This time with the Lord opens up communications so that believers can both listen and talk to Him. Then He imparts whatever they need. If they need hope, restoration or finances, He will deposit these things in them.

This chapter is the culmination of all the things which were written earlier in the book. It addresses being joined to the Lord, as oneness with the Lord brings forth the new season of prosperity. The objective of this chapter is to explore intimacy with the Lord in terms of feasting with Him.

Transition from the Old Order to the New

In the Old Testament, the Israelites celebrated three major feasts: the Feast of Unleavened Bread, the Feast of Weeks and the Feast of Booths (Deuteronomy 16:16). They celebrated the feasts by eating specific foods at certain times. These feasts were carnal activities. The feasts dealt with rules and regulations concerning food and drink until the complete new order was established by Jesus Christ (Hebrews 9:10). He established the reality of the things that the feasts foreshadowed: "Therefore no one is to act as your judge in regard to food or drink or in respect to a festival or a new moon or a Sabbath day – things which are a mere shadow of what is to come; but the substance belongs to Christ" (Colossians 2:16-17).

Jesus signaled a change in the feasts from the carnal realm to the spiritual when he refused to go to the Feast of Tabernacles when others went to it (John 7:2-9). Instead, Jesus came at the last of the feast and spoke about the Holy Spirit being manifested through the lives of believers (John 7:37-39). Jesus referred to the spiritual nature of the feasts. Studying the symbols related to the feasts helps believers understand the intended spiritual nature of the feasts.

The first feast was Unleavened Bread or Passover. The Israelites ate lamb and unleavened bread during this feast. The blood of the lamb was applied to the doorposts of their houses so that the death angel would pass over them. Leaven represents sin or hypocrisy: "Therefore let us celebrate the feast, not with old leaven, nor with the leaven of malice and wickedness, but with the unleavened bread of sincerity and truth" (1 Corinthians 5:8). Jesus is the spotless Lamb of God (John 1:29, 36) and the pure Bread of Life (John 6:35, 48, 51). Jesus is Passover for all those who believe (1 Corinthians 5:7). His blood can be applied to believers' lives by being born again and by recognizing the sacrifice of Jesus as the Lamb of God. After being born again, believers can continually consume the Bread of Life by studying the word of God.

The second feast is the Feast of Weeks which ends at Pentecost. The feast began at the earliest harvest when the priest waved the first of the fruits before the Lord. It ended fifty days later at the end of the harvest. Jesus Christ is the first fruits (1 Corinthians 15:23). He was raised first and every believer will be raised in turn. The Feast of Weeks symbolizes continual harvest and hence abundance for believers. Pentecost represents the power of the Holy Spirit operating through the lives of believers.

The third feast is Booths or Tabernacles. This was the final feast of the year. Two goats were used in the feast for the sins of the people (Leviticus 16). The first was a scapegoat which took the blame for the sins of God's people. The second goat was sacrificed so that its blood could be carried by the High Priest into the Most Holy Place to cover the people's sins. The High Priest entered into the Most Holy Place only once a year during this feast. Jesus symbolizes both goats. He became the scapegoat by being punished for our sins (2 Corinthians 5:21). After His death and resurrection, Jesus carried His own blood as High Priest into the Most Holy Place in heaven (Hebrews 9:11-14). His blood purifies believers' consciences so that they can effectively serve God. This feast symbolizes that each believer can become the dwelling place – the booth or tabernacle – for God (1 Corinthians 6:19; 2 Corinthians 6:16).

The New Order of Feasts

The Father has prepared a wonderful feast for the family to honor His Son, Jesus (Matthew 22:1-14; Luke 14:15-24). The food includes the choicest meats, bread, and all the fine trimmings. Drinks include the best wine and milk. This food and drink nourish your eternal life (John 6:27). The table is set, and everything is prepared.

The Invitations

The invitations for the guests are being sent. Many people are invited to the feast; both the good and the evil (Matthew 22:10). No one is being overlooked or excluded (Isaiah 55:1). Even the poor, crippled, blind and lame are invited (Luke 14:21). "And the master said to the slave, 'Go out into the highways and along the hedges, and compel them to come in so that my house may be filled'" (Luke 14:23). The invitations declare that everything is ready now, so come to the feast (Matthew 22:4; Luke 14:17). It is a blessing just to be invited to the feast (Revelation 19:9).

Some people refuse their invitations because they are busy with carnal things. They either pay no attention to the invitation or mistreat those servants who bring it (Matthew 22:5-6). There is more at stake concerning the invitation than they realize. Their families, and even their cities, could be cursed as a result of their decisions not to attend the feast (Matthew 22:7). The critical issue is whether you will accept the invitation to feast with the Lord.

It is important to be prepared and properly dressed for the feast. One man who attended the feast without the proper clothing has already been thrown out of the banquet hall (Matthew 22:11-13). "For all of you who were baptized into Christ have clothed yourselves with Christ" (Galatians 3:27). Since the feast is a holy convocation, the whole armor of God is in order (Ephesians 6:13-18). This clothing includes salvation, faith, truth, and righteousness.

True Feasting

At the Last Supper, Jesus talked to His disciples about intimacy with Him rather than just observing another feast day. The essence of Jesus' statement in Matthew 26:26-28 is "I am your feast! Drink My blood and eat My body. But I say to you, I will not drink of this fruit of the vine from now on until that day when I drink it new with you in My Father's kingdom" (Matthew 26:29). The kingdom is here now (Luke 17:20-21). Jesus drinks the new wine today in the kingdom with those believers who seek intimacy with Him.

People may think about the marriage supper of the Lamb in carnal terms (Revelation 19:9). But that feast is spiritual and not carnal in any sense. It cannot be understood through the carnal mind. Feasting with the Lord is an intimate activity. It involves leaving the carnal realm to embrace the spiritual realm.

Everything needed is provided, which is a good description of abundance. Jesus made provision through His being the Lamb of

God and the Bread of Life. In Him believers have all things (Romans 8:32). He brings believers into a wealthy place by Him, so that they can enjoy each other.

Yearnings of the Spirit Man

When a person is born again, or saved, his/her spirit man is recreated with new life (John 3:3; Romans 6:4). Then the spirit man must be nurtured and strengthened. Without spiritual food and development, the spirit man remains malnourished, impoverished and imprisoned. The word of God is the food for spiritual growth (1 Peter 2:2). Prayer is also needed to develop the spirit man.

After the spirit is recreated then the soul – the mind, will and emotions – can be renewed and saved (Ephesians 4:23-24). It takes the anointed word of God to renew the mind and save the soul (James 1:21). Until the mind is renewed, every believer experiences a struggle between the recreated spirit and the old nature – or flesh – which wants to control the spirit man (Galatians 5:17). When the flesh rules the spirit man, the result is carnality. The carnal mind is hostile towards God (Romans 8:7). When the mind is renewed so that the spirit man rules the flesh, there will be oneness in spirit and soul.

Who really knows the spirit man? There are a few important things known about the spirit man. First, the spirit man yearns for heavenly things rather than for earthly or mundane things. The spirit man will seek those things above where Christ is seated at the right hand of God (Colossians 3:1-2). The spirit man yearns for fellowship with the Lord.

Second, the spirit man must be liberated to fulfill purpose and destiny. It takes the Holy Spirit to free the spirit man: "Now the Lord is the Spirit, and where the Spirit of the Lord is, there is liberty" (2 Corinthians 3:17). The more a believer communes with the Holy Spirit, the freer the spirit man becomes. A good example to help you understand the concept of freeing the spirit man is the resurrection of Lazarus from the dead (John 11:41-44). After Jesus called Lazarus from death to life, Lazarus still had to be loosed from the grave clothes. Likewise, people who experience the new birth sill have to be loosed from all the things that would otherwise keep them in bondage. Loose the spirit man and let him go free.

Third, the spirit man's general purpose is to yield fruit for the Lord: "But the fruit of the Spirit is love, joy, peace, patience, kindness, goodness, faithfulness, gentleness, self-control; against such things there is no law" (Galatians 5:22-23). When believers catch hold of what their spirit man says, then their carnal mind becomes renewed and fruitful.

Prayer is critical for releasing the spirit man. Both the Old and New Testaments are full of many powerful prayers that God heard and answered. Consider the prayers of Abraham, Moses, David, Elijah and Daniel that the Lord answered and, in many cases, is still answering (Genesis 20:17; Deuteronomy 9:26; 1 Kings 18:36-38; Psalm 72:18-20; Daniel 6:10). Jesus prayed for believers in all generations in His priestly prayer before His crucifixion and resurrection (John 17:6-26). Many of Paul's prayers have become model prayers for believers (Ephesians 1:15-23; 3:14-21). Believers can operate a vibrant prayer life by studying the prayers shown in the word of God. However, just repeating these prayers does not ensure that the spirit man will be brought forth in his fullness. Reliance on the Holy Spirit is needed for the full development of the spirit man.

The eighth chapter of Romans contrasts the carnal man and the spirit man. In that chapter, Paul explains that the intellectual or carnal mind cannot know what should be prayed in order to bring forth the spirit man in his fullness: "For we do not know what prayer to offer nor how to offer it worthily" (Romans 8:26b AMP). From this verse it is clear that believers cannot have the intellectual knowledge concerning how to pray or for what to pray in order to liberate the spirit man. The spirit man hungers for things that the intellectual mind cannot understand. Believers do not know for what their spirit hungers. The spirit man understands things that the intellectual mind does not understand. In particular, the spirit man can have an understanding of a believer's purpose and destiny that the carnal mind cannot comprehend. "For who among men knows the thoughts of a man except the spirit of the man which is in him?" (1 Corinthians 2:11a). The development and release of the spirit man is important for purpose and destiny to be fulfilled.

Pray With Understanding

Strategic prayer releases the spirit man. When Jesus prayed, He was already communing spirit to spirit. When the disciples asked to be taught how to pray in Luke 11:1, they were not at the same point in life as Jesus. Jesus gave the disciples the Lord's Prayer as a precursor to the outpouring of the Holy Spirit. This prayer has all the spiritual elements needed by the spirit man. It continues to be a precursor for Christians before they receive the Holy Spirit and are able to pray in the spirit:

> Father, hallowed be Your name; Your kingdom come. Give us each day our daily bread. And forgive us our sins, for we ourselves also forgive everyone who is indebted to us. And lead us not into temptation. (Luke 11:2b-4)

In general, the spirit desires and hungers for the things expressed in the Lord's Prayer. First, the prayer connects the spirit man with his family origins. Since his Father is the holy God in heaven, the spirit man is holy, godly and part of the universal family in heaven and earth. Second, it projects the Father's kingdom upon the earth. There is no difference between His kingdom in heaven and His kingdom on earth. Third, it makes daily provision for the spirit man. Fourth, it establishes forgiveness as the environment in which the spirit man lives and thrives. Fifth, it sets the pathway for the spirit man as righteousness.

The Lord's Prayer is greatly misunderstood by Christians. Many people mindlessly repeat the prayer without knowing what results to expect. Consequently, they do not see the Father's kingdom brought forth on the earth. Some people teach that it is a model prayer upon which other prayers should be based. They try to approach the spiritual realm through carnal means. There must be spiritual enlightenment before a believer can effectively pray the Lord's Prayer. Praying the Lord's Prayer carnally would be vain. Explaining it carnally would be vain. Others teach that it is not a new covenant prayer because it was spoken before Jesus' death and resurrection and does not reference the name of Jesus.

However, Jesus is the new covenant, so whatever He spoke is new covenant.

The Lord's Prayer is not to be considered lightly, as being of little significance. Whatever Jesus spoke carried significance. The Lord's Prayer is a part of the word of God. As believers pray the Lord's Prayer, they are speaking the word of God. It is a fixed prayer, which is established and unchangeable. While believers can add to and take away from other prayers, they cannot successfully change this fixed prayer because every part is crucial. Adding other elements would not carry the same significance as these elements. Nothing is lacking in the Lord's Prayer, and everything in it is needed.

The Lord's Prayer activates the Holy Spirit. Jesus spoke about the outpouring of the Holy Spirit shortly after teaching the Lord's Prayer. He said your Heavenly Father will give the Holy Spirit to those who ask Him (Luke 11:13). Believers can activate the spirit man in their lives by praying the Lord's Prayer. Believers can use the Lord's Prayer to help make a transition from natural thinking to effectively praying in the spirit.

Pray and Sing in the Spirit

Praying in the spirit each day can bring what the spirit man needs for that day. Praying in the spirit is a higher realm than praying the Lord's Prayer. However, praying in the spirit does not negate what Jesus spoke in the Lord's Prayer. Whatever Jesus spoke was and continues to be eternal. When believers are filled with the Holy Spirit, they are able to pray in the spirit in order to release their spirit man.

The spirit man has a mind to pray and a mind to sing: "For if I pray in a tongue, my spirit prays, but my mind is unfruitful. What is the outcome then? I will pray with the spirit and I will pray with the mind also; I will sing with the spirit and I will sing with the mind also" (1 Corinthians 14:14-15). Under the guidance of the Holy Spirit, the spirit man can pray the perfect will of God (Romans 12:1-2). Furthermore, the spirit man sings the high praises to the Lord (Psalm 149:6). The limitations of the intellectual mind are overcome by praying in the spirit and singing in the spirit.

Once as I was fellowshipping with Jesus in the spirit He asked, "What do you want Me to do for you?" His question to me was similar to what He asked two blind men (Matthew 20:32). They wanted to receive their sight, so He healed them. His question was like giving me a blank check and telling me to fill in the amount. Afterwards, I thought of many things for which I could have asked, such as fortune, fame, power, etc. However, at the time I knew only one thing for which to ask. I asked that I might see His face. Now I realize that it was my spirit man speaking rather than my flesh. My spirit man was liberated through intimate fellowship with Jesus. My spirit man communed with Jesus and spoke to Jesus on my behalf.

David had a similar experience with His spirit man speaking: "When You said, 'Seek My face,' my heart said to You, 'Your face, O Lord, I shall seek'" (Psalm 27:8). His heart or spirit man spoke about seeking the Lord's face. You should know that your spirit man has different priorities than your carnal man. The spirit man's highest priorities relate to worshipping Jesus and seeking His face.

Jesus answered my request by showing me His face many times. I see His face each time I feed the hungry, give the thirsty something to drink, invite the stranger in, clothe the naked, and visit the sick and those in prison. We have fed, clothed and provided shelter for the homeless, prayed for the sick and preached the gospel of the kingdom to the poor and those in jails and prisons. Jesus said as we do these things to the least of His brothers, we do it unto Him (Matthew 25:40).

Worship in Spirit and Truth

The spirit man, whom the Father created for intimate fellowship, becomes fully engaged in true worship: "God is spirit, and those who worship Him must worship in spirit and truth" (John 4:24). Worship is a place in the spirit where believers can go. It's behind the veil in the presence of the Lord. It's a place of being consumed by the presence of the Lord. Fleshly desires, fears and anxieties are burned up in the presence of the Lord, for He is a consuming fire (Hebrews 12:29). A worshipper's perspective is dramatically changed as the Lord is magnified over worldly situations. Temporal things become less significant than previously thought when the worshipper faces eternity in the presence of the Lord.

One way to help understand worship is to compare it with praise. Worship is a higher place than praise. Carnal Christians can praise the Lord, but it takes a spiritual person to worship Him in spirit and truth. Praise is a weapon. King Jehoshaphat defended Judah from invading armies by sending singers into battle ahead of his own army (2 Chronicles 20:21-22). When they began to offer praises, the Lord caused the invading armies to turn and fight against each other. Judah was victorious because praises were offered in the spiritual realm before its army fought any natural battle. Many Christians think that fast, loud songs are praise, while slow, soft songs are worship. Worship is not a song at all but an encounter with the Lord. Songs may facilitate entering into the worship experience, but they are not to be confused with true worship.

Two things are critical for entering worship: faith and recognition of the finished work of the cross. True worship comes out of faith. A mother came to Jesus and asked for her daughter to be delivered from a demon (Matthew 15:22-28). However, nothing happened until she humbled herself and worshipped Jesus. She demonstrated humility when she was willing to accept the crumbs from the Master's table. When she worshipped Jesus, He noted her great faith and the daughter's deliverance. When you activate your faith in worshipping Jesus, you can receive healing, deliverance and victory over any situation.

Focus on the finished work of the cross. Any worship that is not based on the finished work of the cross is a fraud and an insult to the crucifixion and resurrection of Jesus Christ. It's the finished work of the cross that gives you access to the presence of the Lord (Romans 5:1-2). Lift up the sacrificial Lamb of God. Believers are continually worshipping the Lamb of God around the throne of God (Revelation 7:10-13). The Lamb of God is the temple and the light of the heavenly Jerusalem (Revelation 21:22-23). Proclaim the power of the cross. Ascribe all power to the resurrected Savior and none to any enemy of the cross. Declare the precious name of Jesus, which is above every other name. Believers were redeemed with the precious blood of Jesus

Christ (1 Peter 1:18-19). Plead the shed blood of Jesus over your life and situations. His blood is incorruptible and able to cleanse, sanctify, heal, and deliver. Your worship becomes more effective as you focus on Jesus and those things which He accomplished at the cross.

Believers can expect powerful moves of the Holy Spirit in worship when they deny all selfish interests and fully commit to doing the Lord's will. Then each encounter with the Lord will bring changes in the life of a true worshipper. If nothing happens or changes as a result of worshipping the Lord, then something in the worship experience is not right. Life changing experiences come out of true worship.

One time when I was worshipping Jesus, I began to imagine that I was in a great multitude of worshippers. I imagined that King Jesus was riding through the crowd on His horse. Then the Holy Spirit changed what I was imagining to a heavenly vision. In the vision Jesus rode His horse up to me. He dismounted and started to place His robe on my back. I drew back at the thought of His placing the robe on me, because I did not want Him to do it. He asked whether I had ever read the book of Esther, which explains how the Lord honors a person. The person being honored wears the kings' robe and rides the king's horse (Esther 8:7-9). A noble prince leads the person being honored on horseback through the city. The Lord can honor a person this way. He honored me by letting me wear His robe and ride His horse. Jesus, himself, was the noble prince who led me through the city, proclaiming that I was being honored. When I entered the place of worship where the Lord was truly being honored, He turned to honor me. This was a life changing experience for me. He will also honor you when you enter the place of true worship.

Conclusions

A common thread that ties the chapters of this book together is that prosperity begins as an inward work but manifests as an outward expression. Any issue inside a person that hinders prosperity must be identified and resolved (chapter 1). Some of these issues may be readily apparent to the believer, while others may be revealed over a period of time by the Holy Spirit. Building strong personal relationships with the Father, His Son and His Spirit will reveal the hidden issues, heal the wounds and make the believer whole (chapter 2). Prosperity flows out of the spirit man onto the soul and over the body and finances. Four foundations for prosperity are love, contentment, purity and righteousness (chapters 2 and 3). These foundations relate to the Father and His plan for a family which is conformed to the image of His Son, Jesus.

The Heavenly Father is described as the Father of spirits (Hebrews 12:9), but He is never described as the Father of souls or flesh. The spirit man which conforms to the image of Christ to do the Father's will is called the kingdom spirit (chapter 4). The kingdom spirit has authority over natural situations. The Father brings believers into family where they can be nurtured, equipped and fulfilled as sons (neither male nor female). True prosperity belongs to sons. Then the hearts of the sons are turned to the family, because they are imitators of their Heavenly Father. Following the Father, sons want to give the best off the top for the family (chapter 5). They look beyond present circumstances and begin to fashion the future for themselves and their family. Functioning as sons, they become stewards of the Father's resources, such as grace, rather than independent operators. The sons become good stewards by relying on His grace to supernaturally overcome natural situations (chapter 6). The earth yearns for the manifestation of the sons of God (Romans 8:19). The sons of God know and understand the true riches and walk in those riches. They know the Lord and commune with Him. They feast on His blood and His body. The inward work of the Holy Spirit can be seen on the outside.

The Father is pouring out the blessings from heaven as a mighty river on those sons who have made themselves ready as vessels which He can use. In His ever increasing economy, heaven can be called on to change earthly situations (chapter 7). In the spiritual family, His sons are receiving their inheritance from their fathers and passing a lasting legacy along to their own spiritual and natural children (chapter 8). The family's legacy is impacting generation after generation. The family is being called to the feast. Jesus, who wants believers to partake of His body and His blood, is the new feast (chapter 9). Believers can become intimate with Jesus by developing and releasing the spirit man to soar freely to the highest spiritual level. Then they can truly worship the Lord in spirit and truth.

www.fredandsherrywhite.com

9 780615 343349